PRACTICE BOOK

VOYAGES
IN ENGLISH
GRAMMAR AND WRITING

LOYOLAPRESS.

Cover Design: Judine O'Shea
Cover Art: Pablo Bernasconi
Interior Design: Think Book Works
Editor: Pamela Jennett

ISBN-13: 978-0-8294-2832-2
ISBN-10: 0-8294-2832-1

LOYOLA PRESS.
3441 N. Ashland Avenue
Chicago, Illinois 60657
(800) 621-1008
www.loyolapress.com

RR Donnelley / Kendallville, IN, USA / 04-16 / 5th Printing

Contents

GRAMMAR

SECTION 1 | Daily Maintenance

1.1 **Our friends will meet us at the mall.**
1. What is the complete subject of the sentence?   _____
2. What is the simple predicate?   _____
3. What is the object of the verb?   _____
4. What kind of word is *Our*?   _____
5. Diagram the sentence here.

1.2 **He is reading a book about Dolores Huerta.**
1. What is the simple predicate of the sentence?   _____
2. What tense is the verb?   _____
3. Which word is an article?   _____
4. Which word is a proper noun?   _____
5. Diagram the sentence here.

1.3 **The frightened mice quickly scurried under the brush.**
1. What are the nouns in the sentence?   _____
2. Which noun is an irregular plural?   _____
3. Which word is an adjective?   _____
4. What is the prepositional phrase?   _____
5. Diagram the sentence here.

1.4 **She will give us the keys to the cabin on Monday.**
1. What is the tense of the verb?   _____
2. What is the direct object?   _____
3. What is the indirect object?   _____
4. What is the singular pronoun?   _____
5. Diagram the sentence here.

1.5 **Eric and Mia saw Jim at the movies yesterday.**
1. Is the verb regular or irregular?   _____
2. Is the subject simple or compound?   _____
3. What is the adverb?   _____
4. Does the adverb show time, manner, or place?   _____
5. Diagram the sentence here.

1.6 **I cleared the table and washed the dirty dishes.**
1. Is the subject or predicate compound?   _____
2. What is the adjective?   _____
3. Which word is a conjunction?   _____
4. Is this sentence declarative or interrogative?   _____
5. Diagram the sentence here.

1.1 Singular and Plural Nouns

Most **plural nouns** are formed by adding -*s*. Some plurals are formed by adding -*es*. Some plurals are not formed by adding -*s* or -*es*.

Write the plural form of each noun.

1. chair _chairs_
2. variety _varieties_
3. wheat _wheat_
4. trout _trout_

5. waltz _waltzes_
6. dish _dishes_
7. country _countries_
8. tax _taxes_

Underline each singular noun. Then write each singular noun's plural form.

9. The teams line up while each spectator fidgets on a bench. _spectators/benches_
10. The mascots are a cougar and a fox.
11. I glance at my watch and the scoreboard. _watches/scoreboards_
12. The quarterback catches the football and runs.
13. The green team chases him while the crowd cheers.
14. That small player is incredibly fast and agile.
15. He tackles our teammate and the pigskin disappears.
16. Chaos ensues until a man screams "He's got it!"
17. Our boys are running to the end zone.
18. The running back does a victory dance.
19. It is a victory like this game that builds team spirit.
20. The dentist checked my tooth for a cavity.
21. Can a louse bother a mouse or only bother a human?
22. A lone deer stood still as a statue next to the tree.

Choose four plural nouns from above, and write a sentence for each.

23. _____
24. _____
25. _____
26. _____

For additional help, review pages 2–3 in your textbook or visit www.voyagesinenglish.com.

Section 1 • 3

1.2 More Singular and Plural Nouns

Most **plural nouns** are formed by adding -s. Some plurals are formed by adding -es. Some plurals have spelling changes but do not add -s or -es. Other plurals do not change from their singular forms.

Write the plural form of each noun. Use a dictionary to check your answers,

1. knife _____
2. video _____
3. hero _____
4. potato _____
5. belief _____

6. brother-in-law _____
7. passerby _____
8. sandbox _____
9. tomato _____
10. cliff _____

Underline each singular noun once. Underline each plural noun twice.

11. My father's reasons for planting a garden are a mystery to us.

12. Every winter, he sits with seed catalogs piled by his chair.

13. He orders many different varieties of tomato plants, potatoes, and beans.

14. In the spring, the seeds and plants come in the mail.

15. After he plants them, he complains all evening about his back and his shoulders.

16. He spends long hours weeding the garden every weekend.

17. During harvest time, he picks bushels of red ripe tomatoes and succulent beans.

18. Then he eats tomato sandwiches, baked potatoes, and steamed beans at every meal!

Complete each sentence. Underline each singular noun once and each plural noun twice.

19. I do not like _____.

20. I really enjoy _____.

21. In the fall, I like to see _____.

22. My favorite book is about _____.

23. Eventually I plan to _____.

24. When I was younger, I _____.

25. I want _____.

26. Some of my favorite foods are _____.

For additional help, review pages 4–5 in your textbook or visit www.voyagesinenglish.com.

1.2 More Singular and Plural Nouns

Most **plural nouns** are formed by adding -*s*. Some plurals are formed by adding -*es*. Some plurals have spelling changes but do not add -*s* or -*es*. Other plurals do not change from their singular forms.

Underline each singular noun once. Underline each plural noun twice.

1. Did you untangle your hair with the green comb?

2. I will make your copies after I finish printing these.

3. Raul prefers plain water, but Gabriel's drink is orange juice.

4. Check these problems because these numbers do not make sense.

5. The green apple in the basket will last the longest.

Complete each sentence with the plural form of the noun in parenthesis.

6. Amy Tan was born in Oakland, California, to Chinese-born _____ (parent).

7. She is the author of many _____ (story) and _____ (novel).

8. Ms. Tan's books appeal to _____ (man) and women across many _____ (culture).

9. Her stories often highlight the _____ (challenge) of cross-cultural living.

10. Amy Tan wrote her first book after meeting her _____ (half sister) in China.

11. In *The Joy Luck Club,* the author explores the different _____ (point of view) held by mothers and daughters.

12. *The Joy Luck Club* is divided into 16 _____ (chapter).

13. She has written many other _____ (book).

14. They also explore the relationships among mothers, daughters, and _____ (sister).

15. Amy Tan also plays in a band that raises money for various _____ (charity).

Write a sentence using the plural form of each noun.

16. radio, patio _____

17. dish, shelf _____

18. thief, roof _____

19. medium, video _____

20. goose, mouse _____

For additional help, review pages 4–5 in your textbook or visit www.voyagesinenglish.com.

Section 1 • 5

1.3 Nouns as Subjects and Subject Complements

The **subject** tells what the sentence is about. A **subject complement** renames the subject; it refers to the same person, place, thing, or idea. A subject complement follows a linking verb.

Underline the subject of each sentence once. Underline each subject complement twice. Not all the sentences have subject complements.

1. My oldest brother is a pediatric doctor at County Hospital.
2. The wet newspaper lay at the end of the long, winding driveway.
3. The princess of that tiny country is a college student at the university.
4. Mrs. Green is my favorite math teacher at Seaside Middle School.
5. The fireworks lit up the night sky and filled the air with booms, whistles, and pops.
6. The campfire threw off sparks when John set another log on it.
7. Night crawlers are excellent bait for some freshwater fish, such as trout, carp, and walleye.
8. The seventh-grade class prepared for the trip to Washington, D.C.
9. The girls are members of the traveling soccer team.
10. The winners of the three-legged race were this pair of boys.
11. This former astronaut was also a professor at a nearby university.
12. The people in the newspaper story are heroes and should be recognized for their efforts.

Write whether each italicized noun is a *subject* or *subject complement*. Then underline the noun each subject complement renames.

13. Natalie's *necklace* is made of gold and silver. _____
14. The new rock band is *Seven Penguins*. _____
15. The tart apple was a crisp *surprise*. _____
16. A *raisin* was found on the windowsill. _____
17. This quaint *town* is Four Corners. _____

Write a subject complement to complete each sentence.

18. The bus is _____.
19. His movie was _____.
20. The music was _____.
21. Our class is _____.
22. Many students are _____.

© Loyola Press. Voyages in English   Grade 7

For additional help, review pages 6–7 in your textbook or visit www.voyagesinenglish.com.

1.4   Nouns as Objects and Object Complements

The **direct object** tells *whom* or *what* after the verb. An **indirect object** tells *to whom* or *for whom*, or *to what* or *for what* the action is done. A noun can also be the **object of a preposition** or an **object complement**.

Write whether each italicized noun is a *direct object* or an *indirect object*.

1. I threw the *ball* for my dog.   _____
2. She taught *Milo* to read simple books.   _____
3. We sang funny *songs* as we strolled the halls.   _____
4. Hank gave the *postmaster* five dollars for postage.   _____
5. Millie and Seymour baked a delicious *cake*.   _____
6. Eva bought a *box* of chocolates for her aunt.   _____
7. Josh sent his *uncle* a batch of brownies.   _____
8. Dr. Hawkins stitched the *cut* on her finger.   _____
9. The giraffe chewed the *leaves* on the tallest branches.   _____
10. Our team yelled a *cheer* for Leon after his amazing catch.   _____

Write a noun to complete each object of a preposition.

11. The embroidery on the _____ was done by _____.
12. The rain fell on the _____ and ruined it.
13. We will leave after the _____.
14. We sent a quart of soup to _____ in hopes it would help her get well.
15. We walked into _____ without any fear.
16. Several people travel over _____ every _____.
17. In _____, the leaves of _____ turn a variety of _____.

Write an object complement to rename each direct object.

18. The students elected Helena _____.
19. The team selected Josh _____.
20. The teachers announced the concert _____.
21. The entire group unanimously declared blue and gold _____.
22. Katrina and Josie chose flowers _____.

1.4 Nouns as Objects and Object Complements

> The **direct object** tells *whom* or *what* after the verb. An **indirect object** tells *to whom* or *for whom*, or *to what* or *for what* the action is done. A noun can also be the **object of a preposition** or an **object complement**.

Write whether each italicized noun is a *direct object*, an *indirect object*, an *object of a preposition*, or an *object complement*.

1. Music lovers consider Scott Joplin a popular *composer*. _____

2. Ragtime music started as African American dance *music*. _____

3. Eventually it became popular with the general *public*. _____

4. Ragtime played a *part* in the development of jazz. _____

5. Scott Joplin wrote and performed *ragtime*. _____

6. This music is a kind of march that depends on *syncopation*. _____

7. Syncopation highlights unexpected *beats*. _____

8. This rhythm gave the *music* the name "ragged time." _____

9. Later "ragged time" was shortened to *ragtime*. _____

10. Ragtime became less popular after *Scott Joplin* died. _____

11. Many people declare Joplin's music a great *achievement*. _____

12. He remains the best known ragtime figure in *history*. _____

13. Ragtime music is still popular among many piano *players*. _____

Write sentences using each of the following at least once: a direct object, an indirect object, an object of a preposition, and an object complement.

14. _____

_____

15. _____

_____

16. _____

_____

17. _____

_____

© Loyola Press. Voyages in English Grade 7

For additional help, review pages 8–9 in your textbook or visit www.voyagesinenglish.com.

1.5 Appositives

An **appositive** renames a noun. A **restrictive appositive** is necessary in order to understand the sentence. A **nonrestrictive appositive** is not necessary to understand the sentence and is set off with a comma or commas.

Circle the appositives. Then underline the noun each appositive explains.

1. Sheila, my cousin, works in that department store.
2. I love to visit Pine Acres, our cabin in the mountains.
3. Our neighbor Paul is away on vacation.
4. The black widow, a spider, is poisonous.
5. Mr. James, the principal, is in the cafeteria with his brother, the third-grade teacher.
6. Our dog Blue likes to climb up and sit in my lap.
7. My friend Bindi comes from India.
8. The Nile, a river, is located in Africa.
9. Albert Einstein, a physicist, revolutionized the study of space.
10. Springfield, the capital of Illinois, is my hometown.
11. The actor Katharine Hepburn has won more Oscars than any other actor.
12. Portland, the largest city in Oregon, is wet and rainy most of the year.

Write a sentence using each phrase in parentheses as an appositive to explain the italicized noun. Add commas as needed.

13. Grandma likes to play *mah jongg*. (a Chinese board game)

_____

14. *Pablo Picasso* was an influential figure in the visual arts. (the cofounder of cubism)

_____

15. *Charlie Chaplin* lived from 1889 to 1977. (the legendary actor)

_____

16. Irving Berlin wrote *"White Christmas."* (the best-selling song of all time)

_____

17. *Jim Thorpe* excelled in baseball, football, and track and field. (the great American athlete)

_____

1.5 Appositives

An **appositive** renames a noun. A **restrictive appositive** is necessary in order to understand the sentence. A **nonrestrictive appositive** is not necessary to understand the sentence and is set off with a comma or commas.

Underline each appositive. Circle the noun it explains. Write *R* if the appositive is restrictive and *N* if it is nonrestrictive.

1. Jackie Robinson, the grandson of slaves, broke professional baseball's color barrier. _____

2. The Dodgers retired Robinson's number, 42, in 1972. _____

3. Branch Rickey was manager of a baseball team, the Brooklyn Dodgers. _____

4. The great right-hander Cy Young was a legendary baseball pitcher. _____

5. John learned the Boy Scout slogan, "Do a Good Turn Daily." _____

6. The famous songwriter Cole Porter was named after his mother's last name. _____

7. Chris loves to eat chorizo, a spicy sausage. _____

8. The American composer Aaron Copland meant to develop a uniquely American form of classical music. _____

9. The national poet Robert Frost recited one of his own works at the inauguration. _____

10. Ryan, my brother, loves to play hockey after school. _____

Use each set of words to write a sentence using an appositive.

11. Albert Einstein (genius)

_____

12. African American Olympic champion (Jesse Owens)

_____

13. Pennsylvania (the Keystone State)

_____

14. goal (to improve my soccer game)

_____

15. our sponsor (Ed's Tires and Brakes)

_____

For additional help, review pages 10–11 in your textbook or visit www.voyagesinenglish.com.

1.6 | Possessive Nouns

> A **possessive noun** expresses possession or ownership. To form the singular possessive, add -'s to the singular form of the noun, even if the noun ends in s. To form the possessive of plural nouns ending in s, add the apostrophe only.

Write the singular possessive and the plural possessive forms of each noun.

1. tomato   _____   _____

2. country   _____   _____

3. salmon   _____   _____

4. cliff   _____   _____

5. loaf   _____   _____

6. cross   _____   _____

7. key   _____   _____

8. attorney-at-law   _____   _____

9. Chris   _____   _____

Underline each possessive noun. Write _S_ if it is singular and _P_ if is plural.

10. The new radios were stacked neatly on Sandy's shelf.

11. The scientist crawled into the wolves' den to study their habits.

12. Eli's science project was very well prepared and deserved a high grade.

13. We went from Odette's house to Cayla's pool where I borrowed the twins' towel.

14. The plants' gorgeous coloring was nearly hidden by the thick grasses.

15. The Stevens's yard was covered in the old oak's autumn leaves.

16. The reindeer's hooves thundered as they passed over the tundra's frozen ground.

17. Mrs. Michael's dogs' bones were scattered among the pebbles in the tiny yard.

For additional help, review pages 12–13 in your textbook or visit www.voyagesinenglish.com.

1.6 Possessive Nouns

When nouns are used together to show **separate possession**, -'s is added to each noun. If the nouns show **joint possession**, -'s is added after the last noun.

Write *S* if the sentence shows separate possession. Write *J* if the sentence shows joint possession.

1. Kara and Anthony's paper was about the Great Depression. _____
2. Jake's and Jill's rattles are in the crib. _____
3. Men's and boys' pants are sold in that department. _____
4. My cousin and aunt's house is in Texas. _____
5. Lakesha and Chelsea's poster won the contest. _____
6. Mr. Clark's and Mrs. Williams's classrooms are next to each other. _____
7. The admiral's and the general's orders were given to the troops. _____
8. Lucky and Pretty Boy's birdcage is in the kitchen. _____

Rewrite each sentence to indicate separate possession.

9. Katrina and Josie projects were completed before Michael project.

_____

10. We will visit San Francisco and Oakland museums next spring.

_____

11. Do you think we can borrow Arif and Jaden bikes for the camping trip?

_____

12. I thought Rivu and Bryce paintings showed incredible talent.

_____

13. Chris and Paige dogs were barking all night and kept us awake.

_____

14. Tiko and Onose pencils are blue, but mine are yellow.

_____

15. The president and vice president goals were nearly identical on this issue.

_____

For additional help, review pages 12–13 in your textbook or visit www.voyagesinenglish.com.

© Loyola Press. Voyages in English **Grade 7**

SECTION 2 | Daily Maintenance

2.1 **The attorneys are presenting their arguments to the judge.**
1. What are the nouns in the sentence? _____
2. Which noun is singular? _____
3. What tense is the verb? _____
4. What kind of word is *their*? _____
5. Diagram the sentence here.

2.2 **His sister is the best singer in the choir.**
1. Which noun is the subject of the sentence? _____
2. Which noun is the subject complement? _____
3. What is the simple predicate in the sentence? _____
4. What kind of verb is it? _____
5. Diagram the sentence here.

2.3 **The players chose Max captain of the football team.**
1. Which noun is a direct object? _____
2. Which noun is an object complement? _____
3. What is the prepositional phrase? _____
4. What is the object of the preposition? _____
5. Diagram the sentence here.

2.4 **My friend Nicole is an accomplished violinist.**
1. What is the appositive in the sentence?   _____
2. What noun does it explain?   _____
3. Is the appositive restrictive or nonrestrictive? _____
4. What part of speech is the word *an*?   _____
5. Diagram the sentence here.

2.5 **The women's restroom is near the teachers' lounge.**
1. What are the possessive nouns in the sentence? _____
2. Are these nouns singular or plural?   _____
3. Which word is a preposition?   _____
4. What is the object of the preposition?   _____
5. Diagram the sentence here.

2.1 Descriptive Adjectives, Position of Adjectives

A **descriptive adjective** gives information, such as color, number, or size, about a noun or pronoun. Adjectives may come before a noun, directly following a noun, as a subject complement, or as an object complement.

Underline the descriptive adjectives. Then circle the noun each adjective modifies.

1. Every wonderful vista gave me insight into why tourists choose to visit this area.

2. The quarrelsome children settled into a peaceful slumber.

3. Melanie is so calm and thoughtful.

4. I decided nine guests were more than enough after I calculated the cost of each meal.

5. The young man is exceptionally skillful with this difficult program.

Underline each adjective. Identify its position by writing *BN* if the adjective comes before the noun it describes, *AN* if it comes after the noun, *SC* if it is a subject complement, or *OC* if it is an object complement.

6. Elliot is talented and creative. _____

7. The orange seed pod on that plant is delicate. _____

8. The ripe tomato is just the size for a delicious salad. _____

9. My brother found the golf tournament difficult. _____

10. In the spring the lush green hills invite us all to go for a hike. _____

11. The persistent runner pushed through the crowd to the finish. _____

12. Mr. Lee was short-tempered, but he was also fair. _____

13. I really love taffy, chewy and sweet. _____

Write a descriptive adjective to complete each sentence.

14. I decided to buy _____ _____ watermelons.

15. My favorite food is _____ and _____.

16. We all sat around the _____ table.

17. Tenicia dyed the fabric _____.

18. Kay writes _____ poetry and _____ short stories.

19. Every summer is too _____, and every winter is too _____.

20. The _____ _____ cat stalked the _____ mouse.

For additional help, review pages 18–19 in your textbook or visit www.voyagesinenglish.com.

Section 2 • 15

2.2 Demonstrative, Interrogative, and Indefinite Adjectives

Demonstrative adjectives point out definite people, places, things, or ideas. **Interrogative adjectives** are used in questions. **Indefinite adjectives** refer to any or all of a group. Indefinite adjectives can be singular or plural.

Write whether each italicized adjective is *demonstrative*, *interrogative*, or *indefinite*.

1. *That* necklace belongs to Sophia. _____

2. *Some* boys brought home the wallets they made at camp. _____

3. *What* week are we going on vacation? _____

4. Have you made *this* meal before? _____

5. *Those* flowers grow well in the sun. _____

6. *Whose* laundry is in the washing machine? _____

Underline the demonstrative, interrogative, or indefinite adjectives.

7. Which dessert did you choose?

8. Every child can submit a single entry into this contest.

9. We saw several kinds of kitchen wallpaper, but I only liked a few designs.

10. I know you didn't get these shoes at this store, so which store had them?

11. That teacher told us to choose any desk.

12. Mom asked, "Will you bring me another plate from that stack on the counter?"

Complete each sentence with a demonstrative, an interrogative, or an indefinite adjective.

13. Every _____ days Kyle would ask his mother if he could get a dog.

14. Diego decided to invite _____ of his friends over to play games on his birthday.

15. The police determined that _____ driver was responsible for the accident.

16. Mrs. Holbert decided that we needed _____ day to complete the assignment.

17. _____ set of collectors' cards has Vlad acquired _____ week?

18. I don't know _____ decision to make about _____ problem.

19. _____ lockers still need to be cleaned out for the summer.

20. Will you bring me _____ new notebooks?

For additional help, review pages 20–21 in your textbook or visit www.voyagesinenglish.com.

2.2 Demonstrative, Interrogative, and Indefinite Adjectives

Demonstrative adjectives point out definite people, places, things, or ideas. **Interrogative adjectives** are used in questions. **Indefinite adjectives** refer to any or all of a group. Indefinite adjectives can be singular or plural.

Write whether each italicized adjective is *demonstrative, interrogative,* or *indefinite.*

1. *Which* class do you have first thing in the day? _____

2. *Few* birds come to the feeder in the middle of the winter. _____

3. Is there *another* solution to the problem that costs less? _____

4. *Many* skiers now choose to wear helmets. _____

5. *Whose* shoes are by the front door? _____

6. Which person picked *that* color to paint the living room? _____

Underline the demonstrative, interrogative, and indefinite adjectives in the story.

7. Brian and I wanted to earn some money, so Mom suggested that we rake leaves. Nobody was home in the first few houses we visited. Several people politely declined. Then we came to a tiny house. The yard was covered in leaves. Most bushes were overgrown. "Whose yard is this?" we wondered. An elderly woman answered the door. We knew she couldn't afford to pay us. We thanked her and turned to leave, but then thought that someone needed to help her. We ran home for tools. "You rake these leaves," I said. "I'll trim those bushes." It took us many hours to get that yard cleaned up, but we felt proud of our accomplishment.

Complete each sentence with the type of adjective in parentheses.

8. _____ puppy should we adopt at the shelter? (interrogative)

9. We saw _____ girls at the store yesterday. (indefinite)

10. We can go to the play on _____ night or _____ one. (demonstrative)

11. We took _____ way to the old high school and got lost. (indefinite)

12. _____ recipe do you have for your favorite dessert? (interrogative)

13. _____ brother is in the band? (interrogative)

14. _____ volunteers brought more helpers with them. (indefinite)

15. _____ student is expected to help out in some way. (indefinite)

On another sheet of paper, write a paragraph about a topic of your choice. Use at least three of each kind of adjective: demonstrative, interrogative, and indefinite.

For additional help, review pages 20–21 in your textbook or visit www.voyagesinenglish.com.

2.3 Comparative and Superlative Adjectives

The **positive degree** of an adjective shows a quality of a noun or pronoun. The **comparative degree** compares two items or two sets of items. The **superlative degree** is used to compare three or more items.

Write the comparative and superlative forms of each positive adjective.

1. strong _____ _____
2. efficient _____ _____
3. bad _____ _____
4. slow _____ _____
5. legible _____ _____
6. good _____ _____
7. low _____ _____
8. international _____ _____

Write *P* for positive, *C* for comparative, and *S* for superlative to identify the degree of comparison of each italicized adjective.

9. I truly adore the *biggest* poodles, the standard. _____
10. The little poodles are *cute*, but they do not seem like real dogs to me. _____
11. Our standard poodle, Toto, is *medium-sized*. _____
12. She is *most exuberant* when we first walk in the door. _____
13. In fact, Toto is *friendlier* than a lot of other dogs we meet. _____
14. When we take her to the dog park, she is *eager* to play. _____
15. It is not until I pull out a ball that you start to see her *true* nature. _____
16. I use a ball flinger to throw the ball *farther* than everyone else. _____
17. Of all the dogs, Toto is the *most determined* to get to the ball first. _____
18. She grabs the ball and runs *faster* than the other dogs to bring it back. _____
19. Toto is *more fun* than any other dog I have ever had. _____
20. She makes me feel like the *best* dog owner just because I throw a ball. _____
21. When it comes time to go, Toto is *less excited* to get back in the car. _____
22. She's the *smartest* dog ever; she knows that when we get home she'll get a treat. _____

On another sheet of paper, write a paragraph about a favorite thing. Use each kind of adjective at least three times.

For additional help, review pages 22–23 in your textbook or visit www.voyagesinenglish.com.

2.3 Comparative and Superlative Adjectives

> The **positive degree** of an adjective shows a quality of a noun or pronoun.
> The **comparative degree** compares two items or two sets of items. The
> **superlative degree** is used to compare three or more items.

Underline the positive, comparative, and superlative adjectives.

1. Grandmother is the best cook I have ever met; she's even better than my mom.

2. She is the happiest person in the world when she is in her warm kitchen.

3. In a more somber mood, Grandma told me about her worst disaster.

4. She had chosen the fanciest cut of meat for an important party she had planned.

5. When it was done, she placed the expensive meat on a high counter.

6. While she set the table, her bigger dog, Thor, ate the delicious meal.

7. **Write the words you underlined above into the correct column of the chart.**

POSITIVE	COMPARATIVE	SUPERLATIVE
_____	_____	_____
_____	_____	_____
_____	_____	_____
_____		_____
_____		

Complete each sentence with the comparative or superlative form of the adjective in parentheses.

8. The hexagonal window is _____ (unusual) than the rectangular one.

9. It is a _____ (good) idea to travel as a group than to travel alone.

10. The door finally opened when Brandon used a _____ (forceful) blow.

11. Out of all of us, Kara did the _____ (good) job.

12. I thought Metin's performance was the _____ . (professional)

13. We saw _____ (few) children at the park today than we did yesterday.

14. I think Harold seems even _____ (crabby) than the last time we saw him.

15. I wasn't feeling good this morning, and now I'm feeling _____ . (bad)

16. The price of that jacket is _____ (expensive) than it was last month.

For additional help, review pages 22–23 in your textbook
or visit www.voyagesinenglish.com.

2.4 *Few and Little*

Concrete nouns name things that can be seen or touched. **Abstract nouns** name things that cannot be seen or touched. Use *few, fewer, and fewest* to compare concrete nouns. Use *little, less,* and *least* to compare abstract nouns.

Circle the abstract nouns. Underline the concrete nouns.

1. The bravery of the dog earned it the highest honor in the city.
2. Mr. Johnson was disappointed by the deceit his employee practiced.
3. Hadley showed dedication when she attended school every day.
4. I do not know if curiosity ever killed a cat, but it did cover mine in red paint once.
5. We decided to extend our trust to include Jacob and his little brother.

Use the correct form of *few* or *little* to complete each sentence.

6. There are a _____ iguanas left in the tank.
7. Jan took _____ tissues for her project than Maria did.
8. The company's president has _____ wealth this year than last year.
9. That watering hole always has the _____ antelopes of all.
10. Of all the chefs, Mark uses the _____ amount of salt in his recipes.
11. There is _____ time to play today.
12. We cleaned _____ uniforms this week than last week.
13. This engine is _____ trouble than the one it replaced.
14. The clerk placed a _____ umbrellas by the door.
15. The third-floor apartment uses the _____ heat of all the apartments.

Complete each sentence.

16. The team captain trusts few _____.
17. The dog showed little _____.
18. This month there are fewer _____.
19. Of all of us, Jorge has the least _____.
20. That country has the fewest _____.
21. Since the start of the school year, we all have less _____.

For additional help, review pages 24–25 in your textbook or visit www.voyagesinenglish.com.

2.5 Adjective Phrases and Clauses

A **prepositional phrase** is made up of a preposition, the object of the preposition, and any modifiers of the object. A **clause** is a group of words that has a subject and a predicate. It can be **restrictive** or **nonrestrictive.**

Underline each adjective phrase. Then circle the noun it modifies.

1. Have you read the words of our forefathers?

2. China wanted to protect itself from barbarians from the north.

3. Women in the United States have the right to vote.

4. Let's get together and give her a gift for her birthday.

5. Some plants in the Americas later became European imports.

Write whether the italicized words in each sentence are an *adjective clause* or an *adjective phrase*.

6. The teacher *with red hair* tells many funny stories. _____

7. The statue *of Paul Revere* is visited by millions each year. _____

8. The gift *that I received for my birthday* is precious to me. _____

9. The plane ride, *which lasted two hours*, was far too bumpy. _____

Underline each adjective clause. Then write whether it is *restrictive* or *nonrestrictive*.

10. Louisiana, which was once part of the French empire, is known for its Cajun food. _____

11. Classes that include writing requirements are mandatory. _____

12. Mummies, which are found in many ancient cultures, are a way of preserving the dead. _____

13. The sign that Megan posted read "Do not enter." _____

Rewrite the following sentence twice. First, add an adjective phrase to describe one of the nouns. Next, add an adjective clause.

14. The letter was mailed from California.

_____

_____

_____

_____

For additional help, review pages 26–27 in your textbook or visit www.voyagesinenglish.com.

Section 2 • 21

SECTION 3 | Daily Maintenance

3.1 **We asked them for directions to the nearest gas station.**
1. What part of speech is the subject?   _____
2. What is the person of this word?   _____
3. Which pronoun is the indirect object of the verb? _____
4. Which word is a superlative adjective?   _____
5. Diagram the sentence on another sheet of paper.

3.2 **Three tired puppies were sleeping on the brown rug.**
1. What are the descriptive adjectives?   _____
2. Are these common or proper adjectives?   _____
3. Are the nouns concrete or abstract?   _____
4. What tense is the verb?   _____
5. Diagram the sentence on another sheet of paper.

3.3 **The boy's new black shoes are shiny.**
1. What are the descriptive adjectives?   _____
2. Which adjective acts as a subject complement? _____
3. Which word is a possessive noun?   _____
4. Is this word singular or plural?   _____
5. Diagram the sentence on another sheet of paper.

3.4 **These students will be studying Spanish literature in their next class.**
1. What is the simple subject of the sentence? _____
2. What tense is the verb?   _____
3. Which word is a demonstrative adjective?   _____
4. Which word is a proper adjective?   _____
5. Diagram the sentence on another sheet of paper.

3.5 **Several students in Ms. Ling's dance class entered the talent show.**
   1. Which word is an indefinite adjective? _____
   2. Is this word singular or plural? _____
   3. What are the other adjectives in the sentence? _____
   4. Which word is used as a preposition? _____
   5. Diagram the sentence on another sheet of paper.

3.6 **Which player is the tallest one on the volleyball team?**
   1. Which word is an interrogative adjective? _____
   2. What kind of adjective is the word *tallest*? _____
   3. Which noun is used as a subject complement? _____
   4. Which noun is the object of a preposition? _____
   5. Diagram the sentence on another sheet of paper.

3.7 **Jim's and Bob's robots are good, but mine is better.**
   1. What are the adjectives in the sentence? _____
   2. Which word is a comparative adjective? _____
   3. Which nouns show possession? _____
   4. Do they show separate or joint possession? _____
   5. Diagram the sentence on another sheet of paper.

3.8 **Her report on global warming was very informative.**
   1. What is the compound noun in the sentence? _____
   2. What does the adjective phrase modify? _____
   3. What is the adjective *informative* used as? _____
   4. What part of speech is the word *very*? _____
   5. Diagram the sentence on another sheet of paper.

3.9 **This bedroom has less space than that bedroom.**
1. What are the demonstrative adjectives? _____
2. Which word is used as a comparative adjective? _____
3. Which word does this adjective modify? _____
4. What kind of noun does this adjective compare? _____
5. Diagram the sentence on another sheet of paper.

3.10 **Each job applicant must submit these forms.**
1. What kind of word is *Each*? _____
2. Is this word singular or plural? _____
3. What kind of word is *these*? _____
4. Is this word singular or plural? _____
5. Diagram the sentence on another sheet of paper.

3.11 **The proud parents applauded their children's achievements.**
1. Which word is used as a descriptive adjective? _____
2. Which word is a possessive noun? _____
3. Is this word singular or plural? _____
4. Which word is a possessive adjective? _____
5. Diagram the sentence on another sheet of paper.

3.1 Person, Number, and Gender of Pronouns

> A **pronoun** is a word used in place of a noun. The word that a pronoun refers to is called its **antecedent.** Pronouns change form depending on **person, number,** or **gender.**

Write the person and number of each italicized pronoun.

1. *They* went to the new water park. _____

2. After lunch the tickets were divided among *us.* _____

3. It must have been *she* who bought the card. _____

4. *You* should wear this pair of sneakers. _____

5. Beth gave *me* a lecture about cleaning up the kitchen. _____

6. *We* do not want to wake up late tomorrow. _____

Circle the pronouns. Write *1* above each first person pronoun, *2* above each second person pronoun, and *3* above each third person pronoun.

7. Have you heard of the great ballplayer Joe DiMaggio? Many people say he was one of the best players in baseball history. They point to that stellar ball-playing record attributed to him. But Joltin' Joe, as he was called, also had a sense of grace and privacy about him. He was married to actress Marilyn Monroe, and I don't think that marriage could have survived such a need for privacy. But you might be interested to know that after she died, he sent roses to that grave site for 20 years. I think he really loved her.

Use the directions in parentheses to finish each sentence with the correct pronoun.

8. He is going to the shelter with _____ tomorrow afternoon. (first person singular)

9. _____ got the idea from a friend who lives there. (first person plural)

10. _____ says there are lots of families living at the shelter. (third person singular)

11. Parents need babysitters so _____ can go out for awhile. (third person plural)

12. We'll play games with the kids, and _____ will have fun. (third person plural)

13. We would like _____ to come too. (second person singular)

14. You could ride with _____ to the shelter. (first person plural)

15. If _____ goes well, we hope to go back next week too. (third person singular)

© Loyola Press. Voyages in English   Grade 7

For additional help, review pages 32–33 in your textbook or visit www.voyagesinenglish.com.

3.2 Subject Pronouns

A **subject pronoun** can be the subject or subject complement of a sentence. The subject pronouns are *I, we, you, he, she, it,* and *they.*

Circle the correct pronoun to complete each sentence. Then write *subject* or *subject complement* to indicate how the pronoun is used.

1. Kenny and (I   me) will write the report together.   _____

2. Is it (him   he) at the gate?   _____

3. Was it (she   her) who went to London?   _____

4. Tomorrow Juan and (they   them) will go swimming.   _____

5. It was (he   him) who took the notebook.   _____

6. Ty thought it was Joy and (her   she) who went running. _____

7. The person who climbed the hill was (me   I).   _____

8. (Me   I) went looking for butterflies.   _____

9. (They   Them) took Carmen to the train station.   _____

10. Was it (he   him) who caught the largest fish?   _____

Complete each sentence with a subject pronoun that matches its antecedent.

11. My brother and I play trumpets, and _____ are both in the school band.

12. The Harrison twins play French horns, so _____ are in the band too.

13. Their father is the band director, and we all think _____ is pretty cool.

14. Our mother never misses a concert, and _____ always says we played well.

15. One day my brother broke my trumpet when _____ dropped it.

16. My parents took the instrument to the music store where _____ was fixed.

Write five sentences that describe a family member you admire. Use personal pronouns as the subjects and subject complements.

17. _____

18. _____

19. _____

20. _____

21. _____

© Loyola Press. Voyages in English   Grade 7

For additional help, review pages 34–35 in your textbook or visit www.voyagesinenglish.com.

3.3 Object Pronouns

An **object pronoun** can be used as the object of a verb or a preposition. The object pronouns are *me, us, you, him, her, it,* and *them.*

Underline each personal pronoun. Write *D* if it is a direct object, *I* if it is an indirect object, or *O* if it is an object of a preposition.

1. Val told me the whole story on Monday afternoon. _____

2. The senator from Alaska greeted them on the tour of the Capitol. _____

3. Carlos and Miguel saw her at the library downtown. _____

4. Pat heard that there is an expert on pioneer life among us. _____

5. Samuel could not believe that Mr. Lopez loaned him the pliers. _____

6. Can Teresa stand between Jane and me? _____

7. Even the most familiar teachers did not recognize you in disguise. _____

8. Peter spoke fluent Italian with them. _____

Write the correct pronoun to complete each sentence.

9. I hoped the coach would pick _____ to demonstrate the kick. (I   me)

10. I did not ask why he needed the pencil; I just gave it to _____. (him   he)

11. My dad is going camping with _____ next weekend. (we   us)

12. Paulina gave the box to _____ after the piano recital. (she   her)

13. All of _____ decided to get the teacher a present. (we   us)

14. We saw _____ at the movie theater downtown. (them   they)

15. Armando gave the bike to June and _____. (I   me)

Write the pronoun that correctly replaces the italicized antecedent.

16. Natalie went grocery shopping with each of *her brothers*. _____

17. My grandmother wants to see *my mom, my dad, my brother, and me*. _____

18. Our neighbor offered *Ava* money to mow the grass and trim the hedges. _____

19. The music teacher is married to *Coach Stevens*. _____

20. Carla sang *the song* as loudly as she could so everyone could hear. _____

21. The goal of Carol and *Sheila* was to win the softball game. _____

22. We liked Rover immediately and talked mom into keeping *the dog*. _____

23. Yesterday my math teacher called *my parents*. _____

For additional help, review pages 36–37 in your textbook or visit www.voyagesinenglish.com.

3.4 Pronouns After *Than* or *As*

The words *than* and *as* are used in comparisons. These **conjunctions** join two clauses, but remember that sometimes part of the second clause is omitted.

Circle the correct pronoun to complete each sentence. Then write the verb that has been omitted from the second clause.

1. Little Billy cries more than (he   him). _____

2. Marie sings better than (she   her). _____

3. Craig dances as well as (they   them). _____

4. Does Brenda practice as much as (he   him)? _____

5. Jamal ordered more food than (I   me). _____

6. The children were joyous, and the adults were as happy as (they   them). _____

7. Samuel was more startled by the fireworks than (she   her). _____

8. Willis plays piano better than (he   him). _____

9. Aisha ate more hot dogs than (I   me). _____

10. Chuck took more time to finish than (I   me). _____

Use the chart to write sentences with *than* or *as* followed by pronouns.

	KEVIN	KATYA	MARIA
Games Won	5	5	7
Games Lost	2	3	0

11. Compared with Kevin:

_____

_____

12. Compared with Katya:

_____

_____

13. Compared with Maria:

_____

_____

© Loyola Press. Voyages in English   Grade 7

For additional help, review pages 38–39 in your textbook or visit www.voyagesinenglish.com.

3.5 Possessive Pronouns and Adjectives

Possessive pronouns show possession or ownership. The possessive pronouns are *mine, ours, yours, his, hers, its,* and *theirs,* and the **possessive adjectives** *my, our, your, his, her, its,* and *their* always precede nouns.

Underline the possessive pronoun or the possessive adjective in each sentence. Circle the noun each possessive adjective modifies.

1. I would like to have an outfit like hers.
2. His shirt is the one with the striped pattern.
3. Mine is the house with the blue shutters.
4. I hope our skit is chosen for the school assembly.
5. You left your backpack in the gymnasium.
6. The black-and-white cat is theirs.
7. May I collect yours?

Complete each sentence with a possessive adjective. Use context clues.

8. The jacket is mine. I gave her _____ jacket because she looked so cold.
9. The house is theirs. We went to _____ house for lunch.
10. The collar belongs to the dog. Fido just loves _____ collar.
11. Layla made a dress. We all want one just like _____ dress.
12. Jacob built a table. He gave _____ table to the school for its charity auction.
13. Willem has five cards. He gave three of _____ cards to Tess.
14. Louis and Jaden did a great job. We think _____ project was the best.
15. Alaina won first place. Did you see _____ trophy?

Write a possessive that can replace the italicized words. Then write *A* if the word is a possessive adjective or *P* if it is a possessive pronoun.

16. The bikes are *my family's and mine.*   _____ _____
17. I think the dog is locked in *Collin's* room.   _____ _____
18. Mom is cooking so she won't let us in *Mom's* kitchen.   _____ _____
19. Don't throw away the old blankets; they are *my blankets.*   _____ _____
20. David took those photos in college. They are *David's photos.*   _____ _____
21. The black-and-white cat is *Destiny and Eli's cat.*   _____ _____
22. *Josef's* bag is the one laying in the hall.   _____ _____

For additional help, review pages 40–41 in your textbook or visit www.voyagesinenglish.com.

3.6 Intensive and Reflexive Pronouns

An **intensive pronoun** is used to emphasize a preceding noun or pronoun. A **reflexive pronoun** is used as the direct or indirect object of a verb or the object of a preposition.

Underline the intensive or reflexive pronouns in each sentence. Write whether the pronoun is *intensive* or *reflexive*.

1. You yourself must make this difficult decision. _____

2. We taught ourselves the song they sing at all the football games. _____

3. I myself liked the idea, but it did not pass at the meeting. _____

4. Can you really do all that work yourselves? _____

5. Enrico himself ran to the store for butter. _____

6. Kay laughed at herself and decided to give it another try. _____

7. I decided to take myself to the movies. _____

8. We ourselves preferred the pumpkin pie over the pecan pie. _____

9. You deserve to congratulate yourselves on a job well done. _____

10. Quinn caught himself starting to yawn again and stifled it quickly. _____

Complete each sentence with an intensive or a reflexive pronoun. Then write *I* if the pronoun is intensive or *R* if it is reflexive.

11. We _____ thought we would win the game. _____

12. You all must prepare _____ for the test. _____

13. You _____ should try it. _____

14. I will finish the project _____ . _____

15. Dennis excused _____ from the room. _____

16. The campers found _____ in a bad storm. _____

17. Kate taught _____ to crochet a scarf. _____

18. The dog _____ will star in a movie. _____

19. Jack decided to write a song for the school _____ . _____

On another sheet of paper, write about a time when, as a child, you attempted a difficult task on your own. Use at least three intensive or reflexive pronouns. Circle each intensive pronoun. Underline each reflexive pronoun.

For additional help, review pages 42–43 in your textbook or visit www.voyagesinenglish.com.

© Loyola Press. Voyages in English   **Grade 7**

3.7 Agreement of Pronouns and Antecedents

Pronouns must agree with their **antecedents** in person, number, and gender.

Underline the antecedent for each italicized pronoun.

1. Julius Robert Oppenheimer did not use *his* first name.

2. Oppenheimer led the scientists of the Manhattan Project. *They* developed the atomic bomb.

3. Robert Oppenheimer was a theoretical physicist, and *he* taught physics.

4. He *himself* came from a wealthy family of businessmen and artists.

5. Robert Oppenheimer was brilliant. *He* spoke eight languages.

6. When Oppenheimer needed to present a lecture in Dutch, he learned *it* in only six weeks.

7. The U.S. government established the Manhattan Project in 1941. *It* put Oppenheimer in charge one year later.

8. The scientists successfully tested the first atomic bomb on July 16, 1945. Oppenheimer said, "*We* knew the world would not be the same."

9. Less than a month later, U.S. planes dropped two bombs on cities in Japan. *They* killed more than 140,000 people.

10. The bombs ended World War II, but Oppenheimer said, "The physicists have known sin; and this is a knowledge which *they* cannot lose."

Write the pronoun that goes with each underlined antecedent.

11. Oppenheimer had a brother, <u>Frank</u>, who was a physicist himself.   _____

12. His wife was <u>Katherine Oppenheimer</u>. She was known as Kitty.   _____

13. Their daughter was <u>Toni</u>. She was born during the Manhattan Project. _____

14. Their son was <u>Peter</u>. He was their firstborn child.   _____

15. <u>Oppenheimer</u> himself upset many powerful men of the time.   _____

16. The <u>men</u> agreed among themselves that he was no longer helpful.   _____

17. All had security clearance, but <u>Oppenheimer</u> was stripped of his.   _____

18. But in 1963 the <u>U.S. president</u> himself gave Oppenheimer a prize.   _____

19. The <u>prize</u> honored the man, and he clearly valued it.   _____

On another sheet of paper, write three sentences that each have a clear antecedent and a related pronoun.

For additional help, review pages 44–45 in your textbook or visit www.voyagesinenglish.com.

© Loyola Press. Voyages in English   **Grade 7**

Section 3 • 31

3.7 Agreement of Pronouns and Antecedents

Pronouns must agree with their **antecedents** in person, number, and gender.

Underline the antecedent of each italicized pronoun. Write its person (*1*, *2*, or *3*), its number (*S* or *P*), and, if it applies, its gender (*F*, *M*, or *N*).

1. _____ Chess is a game of strategy. *It* does not take long to learn, but it can take a lifetime to master.

2. _____ Are you going to play the trivia game John brought? I like to play with *him* because he is fair.

3. _____ Players today can choose from many different kinds of games. *They* can choose from very high-tech games to simple word games.

4. _____ My friend Amy has a toy with much more ancient roots. *She* loves her game of mancala.

5. _____ My brother and I like to play a game in the car. Every time *we* see a certain kind of car, we yell "Bug!"

6. _____ Ann and Ron, have *you* ever played with jacks? It takes some concentration.

7. _____ A jump rope is good exercise, too, but *it* requires good coordination.

8. _____ John and Raul are playing with puzzle cubes. *They* are tricky to solve.

Complete each sentence with an appropriate pronoun. Make sure that each agrees in person, number, and gender with its antecedent. Underline the antecedent.

9. Will you and I be partners on the field trip? If so, _____ can talk then.

10. Maggie and Paige have invited their mothers to come along with _____.

11. Grandma adopts homeless animals, and five now live with _____.

12. Mr. Barton gave us the key. After we lock up, we need to take it back to _____.

13. Tenecia is a champion gymnast. We are going to watch _____ compete today.

14. Where are Rivu and Walter? I have been looking everywhere for _____.

15. Have Andy and Ayanna called? _____ were going to call me this afternoon.

16. Do not jump on the couch, because _____ might collapse.

17. Have you seen Thomas? This book belongs to _____.

18. If you see Bryona, tell _____ that Christy and Erica are looking for the book.

19. Max and I are leaving soon, and you can arrive with _____.

On another sheet of paper, write three sentences that include clear antecedents and their related pronouns.

For additional help, review pages 44–45 in your textbook or visit www.voyagesinenglish.com.

3.8 Interrogative and Demonstrative Pronouns

An **interrogative pronoun** is used to ask a question. A **demonstrative pronoun** points out a particular person, place, or thing.

Underline the interrogative pronouns and circle the demonstrative pronouns in the each sentence.

1. Is this your backpack?
2. The waitress asked, "Who ordered this?"
3. Whom did you talk to about that?
4. What is making that loud noise?
5. Which of these is yours?

6. Who is your favorite singer?
7. Do you want to see that again?
8. Whose are those shoes?
9. To whom did you send the letter?
10. What does this say?

Complete each sentence with the correct interrogative pronoun.

11. _____ do you think will win the election?
12. _____ was the score of last night's ball game?
13. _____ will you do this summer on your vacation?
14. _____ of these costumes is your favorite?
15. To _____ should we address the invitation?
16. _____ recipe do you prefer for pancakes?
17. _____ is the best way to get to Oakville from here?
18. _____ is going to read this book at the library tomorrow?
19. _____ of these are you going to buy, this one or that one?
20. With _____ will you share this delicious cake?
21. _____ did you see traveling to the train station?

Use the the directions in parentheses to complete each sentence with the correct demonstrative pronoun.

22. Is _____ the car you were telling me about? (far)
23. I think _____ is the computer that I like best. (near)
24. Please get _____ and bring them over here. (far)
25. I would like to hang several of _____ on that wall. (near)
26. Where can we put _____ so it will not get bumped? (far)
27. Is _____ the one that belongs in the box? (near)
28. There are several, so let's put _____ on the table for everyone to enjoy. (far)
29. How many of _____ will you need to complete this project? (near)

For additional help, review pages 46–47 in your textbook or visit www.voyagesinenglish.com.

3.9 Relative Pronouns

A **relative pronoun** is used to join a dependent clause to its antecedent in the independent clause. These pronouns are *who, whom, which, that,* and *whose.*

Underline each relative pronoun and circle its antecedent.

1. The book that I just finished was written in 1931.

2. The woman who was crying had hurt her knee.

3. A scientist who studies insects is called an entomologist.

4. I heard an aria by Wolfgang Amadeus Mozart, about whom we had studied in class.

5. Walker, which is my brother's middle name, goes well with our last name.

6. The person who has the best math score gets to skip tomorrow's test.

7. The squirrel that climbed the tree was throwing nuts at us.

8. We visited Brussels, which is the capital of Belgium.

Rewrite the sentences to correct the use of relative pronouns. If the sentence is correct, circle the relative pronoun.

9. Abel, who likes to listen to that kind of music, might like the CD you bought.

_____

10. Evelyn Kuo, to who you hit the ball yesterday, thinks you are a great player.

_____

11. Tanner, whom was division champ last season, is on my team this year.

_____

12. My brother, with who I share a birthday, is two years older than I am.

_____

13. Grace, whom I visited last week, says she might be able to come with us next year.

_____

14. The Navajo Churro, which are raised for their coats, are America's oldest sheep breed.

_____

15. My sister prefers cats which have dark stripes through their fur.

_____

For additional help, review pages 48–49 in your textbook
or visit www.voyagesinenglish.com.

Name_____ Date_____

3.9 Relative Pronouns

A **relative pronoun** is used to join a dependent clause to its antecedent in the independent clause. These pronouns are *who, whom, which, that,* and *whose.*

Underline the relative pronoun in each sentence. Circle the noun or noun phrase that is the antecedent of the relative pronoun.

1. e. e. cummings was a poet who eschewed capitalization and punctuation.

2. However, his contribution to American poetry, which was considerable, was about more than the mechanics of good writing.

3. The poet, who was a Harvard student, first published poems while earning two degrees.

4. During World War I, cummings was sent to France, which was an American ally.

5. After the war was over, he returned to Paris, which is a city in France, to study art and to write.

6. e. e. cummings was greatly influenced by Gertrude Stein, whose experimental use of language was unique.

7. A style that combined simple language with unusual grammatical structure changed little over the course of his career.

8. Much like Emily Dickinson, who rarely titled her poems, e. e. cummings's poems are typically referred to by their entire first line.

Write a relative pronoun to complete each sentence.

9. Another New England poet, _____ died the same year as e. e. cummings but was born 20 years earlier, was Robert Frost.

10. Robert Frost's poems, _____ adhered to very strict structural rules, were popular during his life and earned him the moniker of national poet.

11. Many fans, _____ include everyday citizens and literary critics, find his work about simple rural life enjoyable.

12. The American public may never have known Frost's work if it weren't for the people of England, by _____ his poems were first appreciated.

13. The American poet Amy Lowell, _____ discovered Frost's work in London, promoted it back in the United States.

14. Frost, _____ has been given many awards, became famous.

15. The many poems _____ were written by Frost are appreciated by audiences today.

On another sheet of paper, write sentences using each relative pronoun at least once: *who, whom, which, that, whose.*

For additional help, review pages 48–49 in your textbook or visit www.voyagesinenglish.com.

© Loyola Press. Voyages in English Grade 7

Section 3 • 35

3.10 Indefinite Pronouns

An **indefinite pronoun** refers to any or all of a group of people, places, or things. Negative indefinite pronouns should not be combined with other negative words, such as *no, not,* and *never.*

Underline the indefinite pronouns in the sentences.

1. Did you remember to buy any when you were at the store?
2. Both rode their bicycles 50 miles yesterday.
3. Has anyone been able to get through on the phone?
4. We think you need something to do.
5. Jill ate none of her steak, so when she wasn't looking, the dog ate all of it.
6. Several tried to bid on the baseball tickets, but none won them.
7. Some were designed for hiking in the mountains, while others were for the beach.
8. Everyone was amused by the comedian's jokes, and many laughed out loud.
9. Homework? Much of my time was spent rocking the baby to sleep, but I did get some done.
10. Nothing is known about that author, so another might be a better choice.

Underline each indefinite pronoun. Write *subject, direct object, indirect object,* or *object of a preposition* to name its part of the sentence.

11. We are going to a chili cookoff. Have you been to any? _____
12. Most offer a prize to the winner. _____
13. One we entered specified that no beans could be used. _____
14. The rules provided some a great deal of confusion. _____
15. We tasted several and loved them all. _____
16. We were only disappointed that we couldn't have eaten more. _____
17. Mrs. Jackson's chili was preferred by many. _____
18. Nobody had as popular an entry, so her chili won first prize. _____

Rewrite each sentence so that the indefinite pronoun is used correctly.

19. Isn't nobody going to help me lift this?

_____

20. I have never seen nothing quite that expensive before.

_____

© Loyola Press. Voyages in English   Grade 7

For additional help, review pages 50–51 in your textbook or visit www.voyagesinenglish.com.

3.11 Agreement with Indefinite Pronouns

An **indefinite pronoun** refers to any or all of a group of people, places, or things. When an indefinite pronoun acts as the subject of a sentence, the verb needs to agree with it in number.

Underline the indefinite pronoun once. Underline the verb or verb phrase twice.

1. Nothing was mentioned about the dance.
2. Has anything been decided about the transportation we will need?
3. Is something in the closet available for me?
4. Even after all the guests had arrived, no one was familiar.
5. As Henry claimed, all were invited earlier in the week.
6. In our family, everybody volunteers once a month.
7. Was anyone not interested in attending the play?
8. A few of the best writers always contribute poems to the contest.

Circle each indefinite pronoun. Then underline the correct verb choice.

9. Everyone at school (is   are) excited about next week's visitors.
10. We are hosting a chamber orchestra of students, and several (is   are) staying at our homes.
11. A few (has   have) mastered the drums.
12. Everybody (want   wants) to host a drum player.
13. A few (play   plays) the horns, and many play the violin. Others (is   are) cello players.
14. Someone (strums   strum) the harp in the chamber orchestra.
15. I asked, "Does anyone (strike   strikes) the xylophone?"
16. Some orchestra members are from other countries, but all (speak   speaks) English.
17. I asked, "Will a few (sleep   sleeps) on the floor?" Mom said, "No, there are enough beds."
18. Matthew and Onose are cellists, and both (is   are) staying at our house.
19. Neither (like   likes) scrambled eggs, but both (love   loves) music.
20. One (has   have) over 5,000 songs on his music player.
21. Everyone (dance   dances) when he plugs it into speakers and turns up the sound.
22. Now that the orchestra has gone, everyone (miss   misses) the talented and fun players.

On another sheet of paper, match each indefinite pronoun with a verb. Write an original sentence with each pair, using the pronoun as the subject.

INDEFINITE PRONOUNS				VERBS			
nobody	both	few	each	wants	was	are	work
many	several	nothing	everyone	seems	were	helps	go

© Loyola Press. Voyages in English   Grade 7

For additional help, review pages 52–53 in your textbook or visit www.voyagesinenglish.com.

SECTION 4   **Daily Maintenance**

4.1 **Place the dirty laundry in the washer.**
1. Is this an imperative or a declarative sentence?   _____
2. What is the subject of the sentence?   _____
3. Which word functions as the direct object?   _____
4. Which word can be used as a noun and a verb?   _____
5. Diagram the sentence on another sheet of paper.

4.2 **The little black sheep ran behind the neighbor's barn.**
1. Which word in the sentence shows possession?   _____
2. Which noun is an irregular plural?   _____
3. Is the verb regular or irregular?   _____
4. Which words are descriptive adjectives?   _____
5. Diagram the sentence on another sheet of paper.

4.3 **The new president of the debate team is he.**
1. Which word is a subject complement?   _____
2. What are the person and number of this word?   _____
3. What two words function as adjectives?   _____
4. What is the adjective phrase?   _____
5. Diagram the sentence on another sheet of paper.

4.4 **John and Jake like hamburgers, but they love pizza.**
1. What is the pronoun in the sentence?   _____
2. What is the antecedent of the pronoun?   _____
3. Which words function as direct objects?   _____
4. Which words are conjunctions?   _____
5. Diagram the sentence on another sheet of paper.

4.5 **She invited them to her birthday party on Saturday.**
1. What is the subject of the sentence? _____
2. Which word functions as a direct object? _____
3. Is this word singular or plural? _____
4. Which word is a possessive adjective? _____
5. Diagram the sentence on another sheet of paper.

4.6 **The beautiful portrait above the fireplace is hers.**
1. What are the nouns in the sentence? _____
2. Which word is a possessive pronoun? _____
3. What is the adjective phrase? _____
4. Which word is an adjective? _____
5. Diagram the sentence on another sheet of paper.

4.7 **We gave her a bouquet of flowers and eight pink balloons.**
1. What are the adjectives in the sentence? _____
2. Which word is a subject pronoun? _____
3. Which word is an object pronoun? _____
4. Which nouns are used as direct objects? _____
5. Diagram the sentence on another sheet of paper.

4.8 **These are the photographs from my trip to Paris.**
1. Which word is a demonstrative pronoun? _____
2. Does this word refer to something near or far? _____
3. What is the possessive adjective? _____
4. What are the common nouns in the sentence? _____
5. Diagram the sentence on another sheet of paper.

4.9 **Which of the used cars did they buy?**
1. Is this sentence interrogative or imperative?   _____
2. Which word is an interrogative pronoun?   _____
3. Which word is a subject pronoun?   _____
4. Which word functions as an adjective?   _____
5. Diagram the sentence on another sheet of paper.

4.10 **Everyone in the choir will perform at the holiday concert.**
1. What is the verb phrase in the sentence?   _____
2. Which word is an indefinite pronoun?   _____
3. Is this word singular or plural?   _____
4. What is the adjective phrase?   _____
5. Diagram the sentence on another sheet of paper.

4.11 **Each student who participates in the marathon will receive a T-shirt.**
1. Which word is a relative pronoun?   _____
2. To which word does the relative pronoun refer?   _____
3. Which word is an indefinite adjective?   _____
4. Is this word singular or plural?   _____
5. Diagram the sentence on another sheet of paper.

4.1 Principal Parts of Verbs

The three **principal parts** of a verb are the **base form,** the **past,** and the **past participle.** The **present participle** is made by adding *-ing* to the base form. A **verb phrase** is two or more verbs that work together as a unit.

Underline each verb or verb phrase. Circle the auxiliary verb in each verb phrase.

1. We have chosen blue and yellow for the team's colors.

2. Henry and Vlad fixed Michael's bicycle this morning.

3. Dana, Katya, and Timothy flew to Texas last week.

4. I had called her yesterday, but she did not answer.

5. Neal and Abigail could hear the sound of rain on the tin roof of the front porch.

6. My sister and her husband drove me home tonight after play rehearsal.

Write the base, past, and past participle forms for each verb that you underlined in the sentences above.

BASE	PAST	PAST PARTICIPLE
7. _____	_____	_____
8. _____	_____	_____
9. _____	_____	_____
10. _____	_____	_____
11. _____	_____	_____
12. _____	_____	_____
13. _____	_____	_____

Complete each sentence with the past or past participle form of the verb in parentheses.

14. We _____ (give) the bell ringer two dollars for the charity.

15. Constance _____ (sing) beautifully at the service last week.

16. Hope and Kaylee _____ (work) on the assignment all day Saturday.

17. Did you know that plastic was _____ (develop) over a hundred years ago?

18. My dog was _____ (pick) to be on the fly ball team this year.

19. The neighbors have _____ (go) on vacation to Morocco this winter.

20. Chris and John have _____ (eat) their breakfast already.

For additional help, review pages 58–59 in your textbook or visit www.voyagesinenglish.com.

4.2 Transitive and Intransitive Verbs

A **transitive verb** expresses an action that passes from a doer to a receiver.
A **phrasal verb** is a combination of the main verb and a preposition or an
adverb. An **intransitive verb** does not have a receiver for its action.

**Underline the verb, verb phrase, or phrasal verb in each sentence. Write whether it
is transitive (T) or intransitive (I). If it is transitive, circle the direct object.**

1. Aesop made up fables, short moral stories with mostly animals as characters. _____

2. The moral messages within these fables remain relevant today. _____

3. One famous Aesop fable is called "The Fox and the Stork." _____

4. One day Stork ran into Fox. _____

5. Fox invited Stork to his home for dinner. _____

6. Fox served soup in a large, wide bowl. _____

7. With her long beak, Stork could not sip the soup. _____

8. Stork left with a hungry belly. _____

9. A few days later, Fox came to Stork's house for dinner. _____

10. Fox found little pieces of food at the bottom of a jar with a long, narrow neck. _____

11. Stork's long beak fit easily. _____

12. Fox's nose did not fit in the jar. _____

13. Stork just shrugged her shoulders. _____

14. After all, she had learned from Fox. _____

**Write two sentences for each verb. Use it as a transitive verb in the first sentence
and as an intransitive verb in the second sentence.**

15. **drive**

Transitive: _____

Intransitive: _____

16. **teach**

Transitive: _____

Intransitive: _____

17. **help**

Transitive: _____

Intransitive: _____

© Loyola Press. Voyages in English   **Grade 7**

For additional help, review pages 60–61 in your textbook
or visit www.voyagesinenglish.com.

4.2 Transitive and Intransitive Verbs

A **transitive verb** expresses an action that passes from a doer to a receiver. A **phrasal verb** is a combination of the main verb and a preposition or an adverb. An **intransitive verb** does not have a receiver for its action.

Underline the transitive verbs. Circle the intransitive verbs.

1. The lifeguards gave safety lessons by the pool.

2. The little puppy shivered and then shook in the rain and snow.

3. John coughed loudly, but we all ignored him.

4. Every day at the lake, it rained or snowed.

5. Ken and James threw the ball for the dog.

6. Allison studied long into the night and aced her spelling exam.

7. The cats pounce and the kittens leap over each other at my house.

8. The Henderson's lush garden produces buckets of ripe vegetables every summer.

9. My younger brother sets up Civil War figurines and then reenacts epic battles.

10. I can concentrate only when I study at the library or in my room.

Underline the transitive verbs and circle the intransitive verbs. Then complete each sentence with an appropriate transitive or intransitive verb.

11. The child closed his eyes and _____ as he extinguished the candles.

12. Jorge usually walks, but today he _____ in his father's new red car

13. Please tell me, did you _____ the new movie this weekend?

14. Grandma Ethel _____ and hugs us every time she visits.

15. Tina _____ the dust out of her eyes, so she avoided a scratch to her cornea.

16. I _____ the decrepit car as it backfired from three blocks away.

17. Ralph trembles because he will _____ from the 10-meter platform.

18. John _____ the song confidently because he knew all the words.

19. Uncle Albert always _____, and he sleeps well a result.

20. She _____ and the dogs ran to her immediately.

On another sheet of paper, write about some typical things you and your family do over a weekend. Then circle the transitive verbs and underline the intransitive verbs you used.

For additional help, review pages 60–61 in your textbook or visit www.voyagesinenglish.com.

Section 4 • 43

4.3 Troublesome Verbs

Troublesome verbs are those with similar pronunciations and spellings, but with different meanings and usage. These verb pairs are often confused.

Circle the verbs that correctly complete the sentences.

1. He (lied   laid) the wood in the fireplace.
2. I think I will (sit   set) here and rest for a while.
3. Please (let   leave) your shoes by the door.
4. You can (set   sit) that glass over there on the counter.
5. The sun (rose   raised) at 6:30 this morning.
6. The waves (raised   rose) above the dock during the storm.
7. (Let   Leave) Satsu sit by the window.
8. Please do not (rise   raise) your hands from the handlebars.
9. We watched the steam (raise   rise) from the cup of coffee.
10. The dog decided to (lay   lie) on the cold tile floor.
11. Did you (lend   borrow) that rake from Mr. McCoy?
12. We like to (lie   lay) on the sandy beach and soak up the summer sun.
13. The cat (sat   set) on the windowsill and cleaned herself meticulously in the moonlight.
14. Mr. Hawthorne (learned   taught) me the proper way to (rise   raise) the flag.
15. (Let   Leave) the video game alone, and please (sit   set) down at the table.
16. The gray striped cat (lay   laid) in the sun all afternoon.
17. Will you (sit   set) the bowl on the table and help me (raise   rise) the window?
18. My parents (let   leave) me go to the community center, but when I am ready to (let   leave), they will pick me up.
19. We should (lend   borrow) Amy our extra jacket.
20. Joe and I (learned   taught) how to tie knots and (sit   set) tent pegs last weekend.

Rewrite the sentences to correct the use of troublesome verbs.

21. Natalie learned me how to do the algebra problems with which I was struggling.

_____

22. Go set on the couch and let the poor dog alone.

_____

23. Please don't let your clothes laying all over the house.

_____

24. May Herb and Jake lend our lawn mower and return it tomorrow?

_____

For additional help, review pages 62–63 in your textbook or visit www.voyagesinenglish.com.

4.4 Linking Verbs

A **linking verb** does not express action. Instead, it joins a subject with a subject complement.

Complete each sentence with the part of speech in parentheses. Underline the linking verb.

1. The weather turned _____ last night. (adjective)
2. These sunflowers grow _____ in the garden. (adjective)
3. That person is an _____. (noun)
4. Even though it was tired, the cat remained _____. (adjective)
5. Hector and Jayden are _____. (noun)
6. The fluffy buttermilk pancakes tasted _____. (adjective)
7. The water remained _____ even after the storm. (adjective)
8. The caterpillar became a _____. (noun)

Underline the linking verb in each sentence. Then write the subject complement for the linking verb.

9. The wasps became more active during the day. _____
10. Michael Jordan was an amazing basketball player. _____
11. Plymouth Drive was the street you should have taken. _____
12. The muffins from the bake sale tasted superb. _____
13. The winning players seem terribly nervous. _____
14. The referee remained calm throughout the game. _____
15. In the fairy tale, the lizard is actually a prince. _____
16. Lindsey feels excited about her tryout. _____

Underline the verb in each sentence. Then write whether that verb is transitive (T), intransitive (I), or linking (L).

17. Our family owns a set of dirt bikes. _____
18. My dad taught us the rules of the sport long ago. _____
19. My dirt bike is green with yellow flames. _____
20. Just about every weekend, we race in the desert. _____
21. My older sister is the best rider of us all. _____

For additional help, review pages 64–65 in your textbook or visit www.voyagesinenglish.com.

Section 4 • 45

4.5 Active and Passive Voices

When a transitive verb is in the **active voice,** the subject is the doer of the action. In the **passive voice,** the subject is the receiver of the action.

Underline the verb or verb phrase in each sentence. Then write whether that verb is in the active voice (*A*) or passive voice (*P*).

1. The overripe fruit hit the ground with a splat. _____
2. The story is read by the famous actor Melvin Belleville. _____
3. My brother reads quietly in the green chair every evening. _____
4. The bountiful harvest rewarded us all. _____
5. Only the cars were damaged in the three-car accident. _____
6. The stockings were hung by the youngest child in the family. _____
7. All night the watchdog carefully guarded the front gate. _____
8. The fire in the wood-burning stove is lit by me. _____
9. The dutiful mother cat follows her young kittens around the house. _____
10. Seventeen students participated in the trip to Washington, D.C. _____

Rewrite each sentence by changing the verb from passive to active voice.

11. The trunk was lifted onto the bed by Charlie.

_____

12. The memo had been initialed by the chairperson.

_____

13. A new ambassador was nominated by the president.

_____

14. The dough will be kneaded by Ryan in the morning.

_____

15. The team was invited to the awards banquet by Coach Evans.

_____

16. The address numbers were nailed to the wall by a carpenter.

_____

17. The items on the rack were neatly organized by the sales associate.

_____

For additional help, review pages 66–67 in your textbook or visit www.voyagesinenglish.com.

4.6 Simple, Progressive, and Perfect Tenses

Simple tenses reflect the present, past, and future. **Progressive tenses** use a form of the auxiliary verb *be* and the main verb's present participle. **Perfect tenses** use a form of the auxiliary verb *have* and the main verb's past participle.

Underline each verb or verb phrase. Then write the letter that identifies its tense.

a. Simple tense   **b.** Progressive tense   **c.** Perfect tense

1. The tour bus will arrive at two o'clock this afternoon.   _____
2. The icicles melt in the warm sun.   _____
3. Her phone has been ringing all morning.   _____
4. Kyle is learning about the history of France.   _____
5. The pool will be opening the first week of June.   _____
6. Martin's fate had been decided in April.   _____
7. Sharon rode the roller coaster three times.   _____
8. The costumes will have been constructed by opening night.   _____
9. Jeremy was hiking on the Blue Mountain Trail.   _____
10. I have been finished with the test for a long time.   _____
11. Isaiah will apply to six schools in the area.   _____
12. This dog has been trained in only six weeks.   _____
13. The instructor will be giving each of us a schedule.   _____

Complete each sentence using the verb and tense in parentheses.

14. Holly and Emma _____.   (*sing*—future progressive)

_____

15. My friends and I _____.   (*offer*—past perfect active)

_____

16. The plants in the kitchen _____.   (*water*—future perfect passive)

_____

17. Amanda's father _____.   (*know*—present perfect)

_____

© Loyola Press. Voyages in English   Grade 7

For additional help, review pages 68–69 in your textbook or visit www.voyagesinenglish.com.

Section 4 • 47

4.7 Indicative, Imperative, and Emphatic Moods

The **indicative mood** is used to state a fact or ask a question. The **imperative mood** is used to give commands. The **emphatic mood** gives emphasis to a simple present tense or past tense verb.

Underline the verb or verb phrase in each sentence. Then write whether the mood is *indicative, imperative,* or *emphatic.*

1. I can find the information for you.   _____

2. Kate, hold your sister's hand.   _____

3. When was Ronald Reagan president?   _____

4. I did clean my room this morning.   _____

5. You should use more salt in that recipe.   _____

6. Close the kitchen window.   _____

7. Please do not tap your foot, Jack.   _____

8. Juliet does love Romeo from the very first moment.   _____

9. He will read the new book to the children.   _____

10. Emily did run for class president.   _____

Rewrite each sentence in the imperative mood.

11. It is very important to read all the instructions before you build the birdhouse.

_____

12. The workers must be sure-footed and safety conscious.

_____

Rewrite each sentence in the indicative mood.

13. Learn to dance with rhythm and grace.

_____

14. Let's go to the beach today.

_____

Write a sentence in the emphatic mood.

15. _____

© Loyola Press. Voyages in English   Grade 7

For additional help, review pages 70–71 in your textbook or visit www.voyagesinenglish.com.

4.8 Subjunctive Mood

The **subjunctive mood** of a verb can express a wish, a desire, or a condition contrary to fact. It is also used to express a demand or a recommendation after *that* or to express an uncertainty after *if* or *whether*.

Underline each verb in the subjunctive mood. Then write whether it expresses a wish or desire (*W*), a condition contrary to fact (*C*), a recommendation or demand (*R*), or an uncertainty (*U*).

1. If I were looking for a new bike, I would have found one by now. _____

2. I wish I were a star on Broadway, nominated for a Tony award. _____

3. You could check out a library book if you were to arrive before closing. _____

4. Whether she be a pirate or not, that is a fine parrot on her shoulder. _____

5. My little brothers wish they were able to fly like Peter Pan. _____

6. We request that the club be responsible for the home game refreshments. _____

7. If I were sure of the way to go, I would not have looked at this map. _____

8. It's not important that he be at this meeting, as long as he attends the next one. _____

9. My teacher wishes we were more careful about our handwriting. _____

10. Mother asked that we be more considerate about one another's feelings. _____

11. Whether we be traveling to the beach or the mountains, it will be a good trip. _____

12. If I were you, I would take an umbrella just in case. _____

For each scenario, complete the sentence in the subjunctive mood.

13. a student entering a contest

    The student wished _____.

14. a teacher writing comments on a report card

    The teacher asked that _____.

15. an athlete after losing a sporting event

    If I were a better athlete, _____.

16. you make a suggestion to a friend about a purchase

    I suggested that _____.

17. a police officer making an arrest

    Whether the officer _____.

For additional help, review pages 72–73 in your textbook
or visit www.voyagesinenglish.com.

Section 4 • 49

4.8 Subjunctive Mood

The **subjunctive mood** of a verb can express a wish, a desire, or a condition contrary to fact. It is also used to express a demand or a recommendation after *that* or to express an uncertainty after *if* or *whether*.

Circle the correct form of the verb that completes each sentence. Not all the verbs are in the subjunctive mood.

1. The rules require that each player (throws   throw) the ball to the person at the right.

2. Felicia couldn't decide whether this (was   were) the right sport for her.

3. Mom gave orders that she (come   comes) home right after each practice.

4. Mom also recommended that she (take   takes) the express bus from the stadium.

5. She insists that Felicia (call   calls) home if she's delayed.

6. If I (was   were) the team captain, I'd have fewer practice sessions.

7. I would make a good captain, if only I (wasn't   weren't) so busy with my other activities.

8. I'd insist that every player (arrive   arrives) promptly and in full uniform.

9. If a player (was   were) late, he or she would get a demerit.

10. I think it is essential that there (is   be) proper discipline on the team.

Write whether each underlined verb is *indicative, imperative,* or *subjunctive.*

11. Louis Armstrong <u>is</u> an important jazz figure. _____

12. Whether he <u>be</u> here or there, his influence is significant. _____

13. Let's <u>help</u> Mom clean up the mess in the kitchen. _____

14. John <u>is</u> considered a math wizard by most of us. _____

15. I wish you <u>were</u> able to meet my grandmother when she visits. _____

16. I <u>recommend</u> that we refrain from squabbling. _____

17. That dog <u>is</u> an impressive height. _____

18. <u>Read</u> the article about the new library as soon as you can. _____

19. What <u>is</u> being built at that construction site? _____

20. I <u>believed</u> him when he told me the truth. _____

21. She <u>would be</u> on time if she got up earlier. _____

22. I must <u>insist</u> that you be ready to leave at eight o'clock. _____

On another sheet of paper, write three sentences in the subjunctive mood.

© Loyola Press. Voyages in English   **Grade 7**

For additional help, review pages 72–73 in your textbook or visit www.voyagesinenglish.com.

Name_____ Date_____

4.9 Modal Auxiliaries

Modal auxiliaries are used to express permission, possibility, ability, necessity, obligation, and intention. Common modal auxiliaries are *may, might, can, could, must, should, will,* and *would.*

Underline each verb phrase with a modal auxiliary. Then write if the verb phrase expresses *permission, possibility, ability, necessity, obligation,* or *intention.*

1. All the guests might be offered some dessert. _____
2. After the completion of her chores, Pam may go to the mall. _____
3. Sam should take his dog for a walk at least once a day. _____
4. The students must clean the gym after the dance. _____
5. You could take your test in the morning. _____
6. Jason can make birdhouses out of milk cartons. _____
7. We might sing one more song in the winter concert. _____
8. Helen and Emily will collect the donations this afternoon. _____
9. Emmanuel must go to the doctor because of his sore throat. _____
10. With additional free time, we would volunteer more often. _____

Complete each sentence with a verb phrase containing a modal auxiliary. Use the verb in parentheses with the meaning indicated after the sentence.

11. We _____ (plan) the Middle School Fun Night for the spring. (necessity)
12. Irene _____ (make) the decorations for the party. (possibility)
13. Local businesses _____ (donate) prizes for the games. (possibility)
14. Mr. Pearson _____ (be) a chaperone. (obligation)
15. Mrs. Li _____ (bring) extra balls for the basketball court. (ability)
16. Anyone who helps _____ (attend) without paying the entrance fee. (permission)
17. Degliomini's Deli says they _____ (provide) the food. (possibility)
18. Everyone _____ (clean) the multipurpose room thoroughly. (necessity)
19. We _____ (raise) enough money for the eighth-grade field trip. (possibility)
20. We all _____ (be) there to make sure everything goes well. (intention)
21. Our cooperative group _____ (research) the topic after school. (ability)

Write a short paragraph about how students can improve your school. Use at least four different types of modal auxiliaries in your suggestions.

For additional help, review pages 74–75 in your textbook or visit www.voyagesinenglish.com.

Section 4 • 51

4.10 Agreement of Subject and Verb—Part I

A verb agrees with its subject in person and number. Watch for **intervening phrases** between the subject and verb.

Circle the verb that correctly completes each sentence.

1. The computer (is   are) on right now.

2. I (don't   doesn't) play chess.

3. That globe (were   was) made in the early 1900s.

4. Giraffes in the grassland (is   are) easy to spot.

5. My friend (doesn't   don't) understand the geometry problem.

6. You (were   was) my first choice for class president.

7. There (is   are) only two girls in my gym class.

8. A flock of Canada geese (are   is) flying overhead.

Complete each sentence with *doesn't, don't, is,* or *are.*

9. Arnold _____ want to play tennis this summer.

10. Lucille _____ the best swimmer on our team.

11. Cayla and Paul _____ think they can come to the party on Friday.

12. Their parents _____ allow sleepovers, but they can stay until early evening.

13. We _____ happy to be able to help in any way we can.

14. Who _____ too tired to hike another five miles?

15. Main Street Hardware _____ carry trash cans anymore.

16. Casey and James _____ have a pet hamster now that Peanut is gone.

Circle the verb that correctly completes each sentence.

17. The boys and their mother, Mrs. Keppler, (is   are   were) going into the city.

18. The crabs, which come in bright, decorated shells, (does   don't   doesn't) cost much.

19. That map, which shows different climates, (were   is   are) Mrs. Hershoc's.

20. The feet of the arctic fox (is   was   are) lined with fur to keep it warm.

21. This green plaid scarf (does   don't   doesn't) match the shirt's red floral design.

22. Earlier I noticed that the sandy sneakers (were   is   are) under the mudroom bench.

For additional help, review pages 76–77 in your textbook or visit www.voyagesinenglish.com.

4.11 Agreement of Subject and Verb—Part II

Compound subjects with *and* usually require a plural verb. If the subjects connected by *and* refer to the same person, place, or thing, or express a single idea, however, the verb is singular.

Underline the subject in each sentence. Circle the error in subject-verb agreement and write the correct verb.

1. Mathematics are my favorite subject. _____

2. The theater troupe are producing a play. _____

3. The scarf and gloves was on sale. _____

4. Every plant and animal need water. _____

5. Ten dollars are what we paid for the movie. _____

6. The team have practiced all week. _____

7. The cast are rehearsing tonight. _____

8. Neither the cat nor the dogs is allowed in the house. _____

9. The entire group are waiting outside. _____

10. Every avenue and street were covered with snow. _____

11. An anxious crowd were gathering in front of the building. _____

12. The jury are waiting to be seated. _____

Complete each sentence with the present tense form of the verb in parentheses.

13. The track team _____ (travel) to distant competitions.

14. This team and its captain _____ (be) going to Arizona.

15. Jones and Wong Accounting _____ (be) in the office upstairs.

16. Cale and Merlin _____ (run) up that hill every morning.

17. Everyone in the play _____ (come) to the postproduction party.

18. They _____ (say) the instructions for the computer are clear.

19. This ham and cheese sandwich _____ (taste) better than usual.

20. The stained-glass window _____ (diffuse) the light.

21. The football and baseball teams _____ (be) using the weight room.

22. The moon _____ (seem) unusually bright tonight.

For additional help, review pages 78–79 in your textbook or visit www.voyagesinenglish.com.

SECTION 5 | Daily Maintenance

5.1 **The plumber is fixing the sink in the kitchen.**
1. What is the complete subject of the sentence? _____
2. What is the verb phrase? _____
3. Is it a present participle or a past participle? _____
4. What is the adjective phrase? _____
5. Diagram the sentence on another sheet of paper.

5.2 **The Wongs have lived in that house for five years.**
1. What is the verb phrase in the sentence? _____
2. What is the past participle? _____
3. What is the auxiliary verb? _____
4. Which word is a demonstrative adjective? _____
5. Diagram the sentence on another sheet of paper.

5.3 **The librarian found a book about Rome for us.**
1. What is the verb in the sentence? _____
2. What tense is the verb? _____
3. Is the verb transitive or intransitive? _____
4. Is *us* a subject or an object pronoun? _____
5. Diagram the sentence on another sheet of paper.

5.4 **Give me the outline for your research report on Monday.**
1. What is the verb in the sentence? _____
2. Is the verb form indicative or imperative? _____
3. Which word is the direct object? _____
4. Which word is the indirect object? _____
5. Diagram the sentence on another sheet of paper.

5.5 **This month they are volunteering at the animal shelter on Saturdays.**
1. What is the verb phrase in the sentence?   _____
2. Is the verb form indicative or imperative?   _____
3. What tense is the verb phrase?   _____
4. Is the verb phrase transitive or intransitive?   _____
5. Diagram the sentence on another sheet of paper.

5.6 **Our cat Oscar was lying on my bed last night.**
1. What is the verb phrase in the sentence?   _____
2. Is it past tense or a past participle?   _____
3. Which word is an appositive?   _____
4. Which word does it rename?   _____
5. Diagram the sentence on another sheet of paper.

5.7 **The first astronauts were very courageous people.**
1. Which word is a linking verb?   _____
2. Which words does it link?   _____
3. Which word is the subject complement?   _____
4. Is *very* an adjective or an adverb?   _____
5. Diagram the sentence on another sheet of paper.

5.8 **These Fuji apples taste sweet and juicy, but I prefer McIntosh apples.**
1. Which word is used as a linking verb?   _____
2. What are the subject complements?   _____
3. What kind of pronoun is the word *I*?   _____
4. What are the person and number of this word?   _____
5. Diagram the sentence on another sheet of paper.

5.9 **That beautiful mosaic was created by a local artist.**
1. What is the verb phrase in the sentence? _____
2. Is it transitive or intransitive? _____
3. Is the verb phrase in the active or passive voice? _____
4. Which words are adjectives? _____
5. Diagram the sentence on another sheet of paper.

5.10 **The school's band will be performing in the holiday parade.**
1. What is the verb phrase in the sentence? _____
2. What tense is this verb phrase? _____
3. Is it transitive or intransitive? _____
4. Which word is a possessive noun? _____
5. Diagram the sentence on another sheet of paper.

5.11 **Our friend John can play the trumpet and the drums quite well.**
1. What is the verb phrase in the sentence? _____
2. Which word is a modal auxiliary? _____
3. Does this word express ability or obligation? _____
4. Which words are adverbs? _____
5. Diagram the sentence on another sheet of paper.

5.1 Participles

Verbals are words made from verbs to function as another part of speech. A **participle** is a verb form used as an adjective. A **participial phrase** includes the participle, an object or a complement, and any modifiers.

Underline the participle in each sentence. Circle the noun or pronoun the participle modifies. Then underline the main verb twice.

1. Having eaten dinner, Colonel Mansard walked leisurely to the study.

2. He, entering the study, discovered that the silver had been stolen.

3. Did Mrs. Blaine, known for her extravagant lifestyle, take the silver?

4. Mr. Green, stalling for time, suggested everyone sit down for dinner.

5. Humming to herself, Abby seemed unconcerned by any of the fuss.

6. Professor Davis, having arrived late, was flustered by the events.

7. Mrs. Farin was cleared when the written confession matched her alibi completely.

8. A letter copied by hand implicated Mrs. Blaine and her ample handbag.

Underline the participial phrase in each sentence. Circle the noun or pronoun it modifies.

9. Having found the missing homework, Luis was relieved.

10. Workers cut down the trees burned in the wildfires.

11. The man speaking to the teacher is my father.

12. The signs posted on the wall are for next week's election.

13. A cat wearing a blue collar followed me home.

14. Can you reach the books placed on the top shelf?

15. The soup boiling in the black pot splattered all over the ceiling.

16. My favorite contestant was the dog taught to bark "Happy Birthday to You."

17. The hot tea steaming in the blue mug was a welcome sight on a cold day.

18. That silk dress hanging at the top of the display is finally on sale.

On another sheet of paper, write a sentence for each participial phrase. Circle the noun or pronoun that each participial phrase describes.

19. looking through her purse

20. holding the roll of tickets

21. wounded by the enemy

22. formed by stones and boulders

23. followed closely by the excited puppy

24. acknowledging their hard work

© Loyola Press. Voyages in English Grade 7

For additional help, review pages 84–85 in your textbook
or visit www.voyagesinenglish.com.

5.2 Placement of Participles

Do not confuse a **participial adjective** after a linking verb with a participle that is part of a verb phrase. **Dangling participles** occur when a sentence does not contain the noun or pronoun the participle modifies.

Underline the participial adjectives in these sentences.

1. We visited the bustling zoo over the holiday.
2. The pacing lion was popular with everyone.
3. A frazzled father was too busy chasing his young twin sons to see the polar bears.
4. The sleeping koalas were not disturbed by the screaming monkeys.
5. Everyone cheered when the elephants emerged from the darkened cave.
6. We noticed there were no buzzing insects near the bat exhibit.
7. The annoyed camel kept turning its back on the crowd.
8. The patient snake docent helped turn a frightened child into a smiling one.
9. We never leave the zoo without a glimpse of the flying squirrels.
10. This time we made sure to visit the traveling butterfly exhibit.

Write phrases using each participle as an adjective before a noun.

11. scrubbed _____   14. broken _____
12. screaming _____   15. wasting _____
13. driven _____   16. wounded _____

Rewrite each sentence to correct the dangling participle. Add words as needed.

17. Coming home early, the house was empty.

_____

18. Running through the park, a thunderous cheer erupted from the baseball field.

_____

19. Studying the footprints, it was the reason for the missing money.

_____

20. Examining the damage, the book should be replaced.

_____

© Loyola Press. Voyages in English   Grade 7

For additional help, review pages 86–87 in your textbook or visit www.voyagesinenglish.com.

5.3 Gerunds as Subjects and Subject Complements

A **gerund** is a verb form ending in *-ing* that is used as a noun. The entire **gerund phrase**—made up of a gerund and any other parts—acts as a noun. A gerund can be used in a sentence as a subject or a subject complement.

Underline the gerund phrase in each sentence. Write *S* if the gerund is the subject or *SC* if the gerund is the subject complement.

1. Throwing footballs is the best way for a quarterback to practice. _____
2. Jim's specialty is painting with oils. _____
3. Putting together puzzles helped quiet the young child. _____
4. Watching sports is one way that my brother passes his time. _____
5. The girl's favorite pastime is listening to music. _____
6. The high point of my trip was searching in the caves. _____
7. Collecting stamps was how I received my last merit badge. _____
8. Humming a familiar song helped the nervous actor stay calm. _____
9. My least favorite job is vacuuming the hallway. _____
10. Meena's preferred exercise is jogging through her neighborhood. _____

Write a gerund used as a subject or a subject complement to complete each sentence.

11. _____ scientists to ask questions is what Jupiter does best.
12. An important part of the Juno project is _____ us understand the planets.
13. Juno's mission is _____ the largest gaseous planet in our solar system.
14. _____ into the swirling gases is a function of the spacecraft.
15. _____ difficult questions has long been the goal of our space programs.
16. _____ distant planets has captured the imagination of humanity.
17. Many of us are _____ all these facts about space exploration.

Write a gerund phrase to complete each sentence. Use the verb in parentheses.

18. _____ was a great time. (visit)
19. _____ should be fun. (swim)
20. My aerobic exercise is _____. (run)

For additional help, review pages 88–89 in your textbook or visit www.voyagesinenglish.com.

Section 5 • 59

5.4 Gerunds as Objects and Appositives

> A gerund can be used as a direct object or as the object of a preposition. It can also be used as an appositive—a word or group of words used immediately after a noun to rename it and give more information about it.

Underline the gerund in each sentence. Write whether the gerund is a direct object (D), an object of a preposition (P), or an appositive (A).

1. My grandmother enjoys cutting hair. _____
2. Malaya excels in baking bread. _____
3. Calligraphy, writing fancy letters, looks like an interesting hobby. _____
4. Her record of jumping rope is an amazing feat. _____
5. Jared's job, washing the car, is something he likes to do. _____
6. Almost immediately, Sarah regretted losing her purse. _____
7. Maya's new baby loves playing the peekaboo game. _____
8. We will celebrate all patriotic holidays by raising the flag. _____
9. The officer pulled the car over and avoided stopping traffic. _____
10. Ava's science project, making a volcano, took almost two hours. _____
11. With hard work the boys succeeded in raising their grades. _____
12. This recipe calls out kneading the dough for 10 minutes. _____
13. Some college students need more paper for taking notes. _____
14. Her schedule included visiting relatives. _____
15. This task, raking the fallen leaves, takes the most time. _____

Write a gerund phrase to complete each sentence. Write whether the gerund is a direct object (D), an object of a preposition (P), or an appositive (A).

16. I dread _____ because he scares me. _____
17. Cats and dogs benefit from _____. _____
18. Circumnavigation, _____, is an arduous task. _____
19. His keen sense of smell is useful for _____. _____
20. Today we celebrate _____. _____
21. Kate and Henry decided to postpone _____. _____

© Loyola Press. Voyages in English **Grade 7**

For additional help, review pages 90–91 in your textbook or visit www.voyagesinenglish.com.

5.5 Possessives with Gerunds, Using *-ing* Verb Forms

Gerunds may be preceded by a possessive form—either a possessive noun or a possessive adjective. These possessives describe the doer of the action of the gerund.

Circle the word that correctly completes each sentence.

1. (Me   My) agreeing to the decision was a mistake.

2. (Dad   Dad's) cracking his knuckles made me wince.

3. (Dana's   Dana) slamming the door woke everyone up.

4. She did not understand her (friend   friend's) rejecting the ideas for the project.

5. (We   Our) finishing the hallway mural on time was a good idea.

6. (Tim's   Tim) winning the race made him the conference champion.

Write whether the italicized word in each sentence is used as a gerund (*G*), a participial adjective (*A*), or a participle in a verb phrase (*P*).

7. I hope I have the *winning* raffle ticket. _____

8. *Winning* the raffle was a surprise. _____

9. Carla practiced *sprinting* for the big race. _____

10. She was *thanking* her family for their support and encouragement. _____

11. *Sitting* on the edge of our seats, we waited to see what would happen next. _____

12. The clown was *juggling* six basketballs at once. _____

Write a sentence using each word as a gerund, a participle, or a verb in the progressive tense. Then write how you used the word.

13. running: _____

    Word used as _____.

14. shining: _____

    Word used as _____.

15. making: _____

    Word used as _____.

16. finishing: _____

    Word used as _____.

© Loyola Press. Voyages in English   Grade 7

For additional help, review pages 92–93 in your textbook or visit www.voyagesinenglish.com.

5.6 Infinitives as Subjects and Subject Complements

> An **infinitive** is a verb form, usually preceded by *to*, that is used as a noun, an adjective, or an adverb.

Underline each infinitive or infinitive phrase. Write whether the infinitive is used as a *subject* or *subject complement*.

1. To complain is a waste of time.   _____

2. Her wish is to travel throughout Europe.   _____

3. To tell the truth was the best choice.   _____

4. His primary goal is to do the best job he can.   _____

5. To express your emotions is healthy.   _____

6. Our first goal is to visit the Grand Canyon.   _____

7. My plan for getting the role is to practice my lines. _____

8. To swim in a tropical lagoon would be a wonderful thing. _____

9. To snowboard should be quite exciting.   _____

10. The purpose of the poster is to symbolize freedom. _____

Write an infinitive or infinitive phrase to complete each sentence. Write if the infinitive is used as a subject (*S*), or a subject complement (*SC*).

11. _____ was common in the Old West.   _____

12. The goal of many people is _____.   _____

13. _____ is a challenge for many students. _____

14. _____ is often a requirement for success. _____

15. A precursor for victory in any race is _____. _____

16. _____ was needed for combustion to occur. _____

17. Another useful character trait is _____. _____

18. Henderson's primary talent was _____.   _____

19. _____ is key to traveling safely.   _____

20. One way to see the world would be _____. _____

21. _____ is a task for most motivated students. _____

22. A wish I have had for a long time is _____. _____

© Loyola Press. Voyages in English   Grade 7

> For additional help, review pages 94–95 in your textbook or visit www.voyagesinenglish.com.

5.7 Infinitives as Objects

An infinitive functioning as a noun can be used as a direct object in a sentence. This direct object may be preceded by a noun or pronoun. The infinitive and its subject form an **infinitive clause.**

Underline the infinitives used as a direct object in each sentence.

1. The builders wanted to support the roof by reinforcing the walls.
2. The suspect wrote to confess to the crime.
3. John intended to propose to Mary on the transcontinental train trip.
4. The children were taught to tolerate different points of view.
5. Adelle continued to deny any involvement in the prank.

Underline the infinitive, infinitive phrase, or infinitive clause in each sentence. Circle the verb of which each is the direct object.

6. The old cat loved to abandon its toys in the middle of the carpet.
7. The club president needs to increase recognition for the club in the school.
8. Carrie tried to understand the complex construction of the sentence.
9. Rolph wanted to watch his favorite movie over and over.
10. We regret to inform you that your application to Upstart Academy has been denied.

Underline each infinitive used as a noun. Write whether the infinitive is used as a subject (S), a subject complement (SC), or a direct object (DO).

11. The missionaries wanted to build a school. _____
12. My plan for vacation is to read several books. _____
13. To study for two hours each night is my goal for this week. _____
14. We agreed that the best option was to postpone the trip. _____
15. The politician promised to make the public aware of the issues. _____
16. To cross the finish line was my goal. _____
17. When did you decide to administer the test? _____
18. The guests expected to return to their seats. _____
19. The substitute teacher's first task was to take attendance. _____
20. Roger's first task is to find an answer to all his questions. _____

On another sheet of paper, write sentences using three infinitives. Use one infinitive as a subject, one as a subject complement, and one as a direct object.

For additional help, review pages 96–97 in your textbook or visit www.voyagesinenglish.com.

5.8 Infinitives as Appositives

An infinitive functioning as a noun can be used as an appositive. An appositive is a word or group of words used after a noun or pronoun to rename it and give more information about it.

Underline the infinitive phrase used as an appositive in each sentence. Then circle the word that each appositive explains.

1. It was the actor's role, to make the audience laugh, that he accomplished best.

2. Her endeavor, to climb the world's tallest mountain, will take much preparation.

3. Our dream, to visit all the U.S. national parks, will come true someday.

4. Tia's kindness, to help the small child, earned her respect from her parents.

5. Dillan's assignment, to write a short story, is due in two weeks.

6. The country's need, to conserve natural resources, requires everyone's commitment.

7. Miguel's goal, to win the spelling championship, occupies a great deal of his time.

8. The agreement, to share the money equally, pleased both sides.

9. The children's reward, to visit the amusement park, was well deserved.

10. Our objective, to improve school spirit, proved most difficult.

11. The president's oath, to serve our country, is an essential part of the inauguration.

12. My primary focus, to keep from getting seasick, did not last long.

Underline each infinitive or infinitive phrase. Write whether the infinitive is used as a _subject_, a _subject complement_, a _direct object_, or an _appositive_.

13. To allow sweets was more than the nanny would allow. _____

14. Our hope, to walk the deck before night fell, was thwarted. _____

15. The king was permitted to rule the country. _____

16. To suggest cooperation seemed disloyal. _____

17. Julie tried to prevent the captain's escape. _____

18. The cook's idea, to invite Karen for dinner, was a good one. _____

19. Eva's greatest fault, to argue every point, annoyed us all. _____

20. The purpose of the signs was to warn us of the danger. _____

21. Javier strained to picture the next season. _____

On another sheet of paper, write three sentences that each use an infinitive as a noun.

For additional help, review pages 98–99 in your textbook or visit www.voyagesinenglish.com.

5.9 Infinitives as Adjectives

Infinitives can be used as adjectives to describe nouns and pronouns. These infinitives follow the words they describe.

Underline the infinitive phrase in each sentence. Then circle the noun it describes.

1. The time to check the list of ingredients is before you start baking.
2. The group chose this book to read for their report.
3. The company president stressed the need to advertise the new product.
4. Here's a list of the rules to follow.
5. I explained that the athletic director was the man to see.
6. That dog has the talent to track missing people.
7. Mr. Harper devised a system to organize all our homework assignments.
8. Before anyone else got home, Carl made an effort to clean up the mess.
9. At what point in history did women get the right to vote in elections?
10. It was Mother Teresa's work to feed and to clothe people who were poor.
11. The sign directed me to the person to see for the application.
12. The investigator knew this was the case to solve as quickly as possible.

Write an infinitive phrase that acts as an adjective to complete each sentence. Then circle the noun each describes.

13. I know an easier way _____.
14. Sheila is the person _____.
15. The library is the place _____.
16. Mother had a special ability _____.
17. Two brothers made a pledge _____.
18. The man invented a machine _____.
19. We all made an effort _____.
20. He thought of a more efficient way _____.
21. Her creativity led to a design _____.
22. Jack had an idea _____.
23. We raised money _____.
24. The children had a chance _____.

© Loyola Press. Voyages in English   Grade 7

For additional help, review pages 100–101 in your textbook
or visit www.voyagesinenglish.com.

5.10 Infinitives as Adverbs

An infinitive can be used as an adverb—to describe a verb, an adjective, or another adverb.

Underline the infinitive phrase in each sentence. Write whether the italicized word each phrase modifies is an adjective (ADJ), an adverb (ADV), or a verb (V).

1. She was *nervous* to meet her grandparents. _____
2. Cole *strained* to lift the weights. _____
3. Librarians *check* to see if books are returned in good condition. _____
4. We talked *quietly* to avoid waking the baby. _____
5. The farmer is *happy* to see the rain come down. _____
6. Eli was *ecstatic* to ride on the team bus. _____
7. Together we *worked* to clean the kitchen. _____
8. Nina *had arrived* to try a new recipe. _____
9. I reviewed my essay *carefully* to check for any errors. _____
10. The fitness test was too *easy* to give to the coach. _____
11. We *struggled* to stand up in the wind. _____
12. Those children are old *enough* to know better. _____

Underline the infinitive phrase in each sentence. Write whether the infinitive phrase is used as a noun (N), an adjective (ADJ), or an adverb (ADV).

13. The year-end trip will be to camp by the lake. _____
14. The doctors were ready to handle any emergency. _____
15. The people to help right now are the ones waiting in line. _____
16. Mom and Dad planned a party to celebrate their anniversary. _____
17. Our goal was to help the victims as much as possible. _____
18. To raise money before the invoice was due is now our only hope. _____
19. Jacob and Julie worked together to produce a first-place project. _____
20. The band was so proud to win the competition. _____

On another sheet of paper, write three sentences. Use an infinitive phrase as a noun in the first sentence, as an adjective in the second sentence, and as an adverb in the third sentence.

For additional help, review pages 102–103 in your textbook or visit www.voyagesinenglish.com.

Name _____ Date _____

5.11 Hidden and Split Infinitives

> Sometimes infinitives appear in sentences without the *to*. Such infinitives are called **hidden infinitives.** An adverb placed between *to* and the verb results in a **split infinitive.** Good writers avoid split infinitives.

Underline the hidden infinitive in each sentence.

1. The runner felt his heart race as he listened for the starting gun.
2. The lost skier dared hope that the droning sound was a rescue plane.
3. When the scared boy saw his father slowly appear out of the fog, he sobbed with relief.
4. Our art teacher made us work slowly and carefully on the pencil sketches.
5. The cat let me help her out of the tight collar.
6. Emil watched the surgeon wipe the area clean.
7. The volunteers helped us learn our lines for the school play.
8. We did not dare take more than we needed.
9. Caleb heard the frogs croak right outside his window.
10. My mom let me go to the Middle School Fun Night, and I had a great time.

Underline the split infinitive in each sentence. Rewrite each sentence to eliminate the split infinitive.

11. I need to consistently keep memorizing these new vocabulary words.

    _____

12. The girls don't expect to quickly find their missing video game.

    _____

13. Kate hopes to eventually write a best-selling novel.

    _____

14. I managed to efficiently use the soap so that it lasted the entire trip.

    _____

15. The server learned to carefully handle the food to avoid cross-contamination.

    _____

16. The child wanted to effectively spin the swing so that all the water spun off.

    _____

© Loyola Press. Voyages in English   Grade 7

For additional help, review pages 104–105 in your textbook or visit www.voyagesinenglish.com.

Section 5 • 67

5.11 Hidden and Split Infinitives

Sometimes infinitives appear in sentences without the *to*. Such infinitives are called **hidden infinitives.** An adverb placed between *to* and the verb results in a **split infinitive.** Good writers avoid split infinitives.

Underline the hidden infinitive in each sentence.

1. The boy watched the toy boat sink slowly into the lake.

2. I did nothing but lay in the hammock all day.

3. Carl made me write thank-you notes to all my relatives.

4. I dared not forget Miss Delgado on the list of people to invite.

5. We watched the fireworks explode in the night sky.

Indicate with a caret (∧) where the adverb in parentheses belongs in each sentence.

6. We decided to continue to scoop water from the leaky boat. (rapidly)

7. The lion wanted to escape back into the jungle. (stealthily)

8. The librarian knew to handle the rare book with gloves. (not surprisingly)

9. I prefer to drive, but I don't mind being stuck in traffic if I'm in my car. (speedily)

10. Heber tried to study, but all he could think about was the party tomorrow. (intently)

11. Dad tried to start the car, but in the frigid temperatures, the battery had died. (doggedly)

12. Abigail started to apologize but then wondered if she was really wrong. (automatically)

13. Hutch and I didn't need to go home that way, but it did seem faster. (actually)

14. I hate to leave Mr. Peterson's class because it is so much fun. (genuinely)

Circle each hidden infinitive and underline each split infinitive in the paragraph. On another sheet of paper, rewrite the sentences to eliminate the split infinitives.

    The last week of classes was a busy one. The students in Mr. Gray's class did nothing but study all day long. They wanted to fully understand the material for the final exam. Some students already felt well prepared. These students need not take all their textbooks home each night. Mr. Gray gave Jessica a special award. She had learned to confidently speak in front of the class. On Friday morning the class needed to attentively listen to the principal's announcements. The students hoped to quickly leave campus on their last day of school.

For additional help, review pages 104–105 in your textbook or visit www.voyagesinenglish.com.

SECTION 6   Daily Maintenance

6.1 **The frightened kittens hid inside the cardboard box.**
   1. What is the complete subject of the sentence? _____
   2. Is the verb regular or irregular? _____
   3. Which words are adjectives? _____
   4. Which word is a participial adjective? _____
   5. Diagram the sentence on another sheet of paper.

6.2 **Drawing silly cartoons is Jake's favorite activity.**
   1. What is the gerund phrase? _____
   2. Is it used as a subject or a subject complement? _____
   3. Which word is the object of the gerund? _____
   4. How is the word *activity* used in the sentence? _____
   5. Diagram the sentence on another sheet of paper.

6.3 **You can support our cause by donating school supplies.**
   1. What is the verb or verb phrase? _____
   2. What is the gerund? _____
   3. How is the gerund phrase used in the sentence? _____
   4. What is the direct object? _____
   5. Diagram the sentence on another sheet of paper.

6.4 **An internship is a great way to learn about a career.**
1. What is the infinitive phrase? _____
2. Is it used as an adjective or an adverb? _____
3. Which word does the infinitive phrase describe? _____
4. How is the word *way* used in the sentence? _____
5. Diagram the sentence on another sheet of paper.

6.5 **The job of the proofreader is to find any mistakes.**
1. What is the infinitive phrase? _____
2. Is it used as a subject or a subject complement? _____
3. What is the adjective phrase? _____
4. What kind of adjective is the word *any*? _____
5. Diagram the sentence on another sheet of paper.

© Loyola Press. Voyages in English **Grade 7**

6.1   Types of Adverbs

An **adverb** is a word that describes a verb, an adjective, or another adverb.

Underline the adverbs and circle the word each adverb describes.

1. Cari has not decided where she will go to summer camp.
2. Scott and Julie hopped impatiently in the frigid air while waiting for the bus.
3. Sissy ran inside to escape the dog that was annoying her.
4. We were growing increasingly concerned about the weather.
5. The mail carrier arrived promptly every day at noon.
6. Kaitlyn and Zoe said the movie was rather disappointing.
7. Hector carefully replaced the face of the broken watch.
8. Natalie did indeed arrive early for the first class.

Underline the adverb in each sentence. Write *affirmation, degree, manner, negation, place,* or *time* to identify the type of adverb.

9. Socrates was indeed a Greek philosopher and a teacher.   _____
10. He would usually teach a student through questions.   _____
11. His questions were carefully presented to his students.   _____
12. Athenians cleverly nicknamed him "the Gadfly."   _____
13. Eventually his views became unpopular.   _____
14. Socrates was fully condemned for his views.   _____
15. Plato diligently recorded much of what we know of Socrates.   _____

Complete each sentence with the type of adverb indicated in parentheses.

16. All the adults ran _____ when they heard the sirens. (place)
17. The detective walked _____ down the dark street. (manner)
18. He had _____ forgotten his wallet. (negation)
19. That necktie is _____ colorful. (degree)
20. Most of the wedding guests arrived at the church _____. (time)
21. Charlie will do his homework _____. (time)
22. The get-well card _____ made the patient smile. (affirmation)
23. The gymnast grasped the high bar _____. (manner)
24. _____, you do not need an umbrella. (negation)
25. Diane looked _____ to see her mom waving from the window. (place)

For additional help, review pages 110–111 in your textbook
or visit www.voyagesinenglish.com.

6.2 Interrogative Adverbs and Adverbial Nouns

An **interrogative adverb** is an adverb used to ask a question. An **adverbial noun** is a noun that acts as an adverb by describing a verb. Adverbial nouns usually express *time, distance, measure, value,* or *direction.*

Identify the italicized word in each sentence by writing *IA* (interrogative adverb) or *AN* (adverbial noun). Then write what each adverbial noun expresses.

1. *Where* was the first radar device used? _____ _____
2. *How* was the Panama Canal built? _____ _____
3. The church bells ring every *hour.* _____ _____
4. To get to the park, turn *east* on Main Street. _____ _____
5. Alex runs many *miles* every day. _____ _____
6. *Why* was the letter returned? _____ _____
7. The book I purchased dates back some 50 *years.* _____ _____
8. *When* did the first human walk on the moon? _____ _____
9. The puppy weighed four *pounds.* _____ _____
10. The winning ticket cost only one *dollar.* _____ _____

Complete each sentence with an interrogative adverb.

11. _____ can we fix this broken lamp?

12. _____ do you think I left my homework assignment?

13. _____ are we going to fit all this stuff back in the box?

14. _____ did you tell Dad we would be ready to be picked up?

15. _____ are we stopping at the store on the way home?

Complete each sentence with an adverbial noun that expresses the quality indicated in parentheses.

16. Our family traveled _____ to go to the family reunion. (direction)

17. For the fund-raiser we walked 20 _____. (distance)

18. We must wait six more _____ until the assignment is finished. (time)

19. He decided it was not worth it to spend 50 _____ on the ticket. (value)

20. This tiny bird weighs only nine _____. (measure)

21. The bookshelf is eight _____ tall, so it will fit in the room. (measure)

22. It took five _____ for the runner to complete the mile run. (time)

For additional help, review pages 112–113 in your textbook or visit www.voyagesinenglish.com.

6.3 Comparative and Superlative Adverbs

Some adverbs can be compared. These adverbs have **comparative** and **superlative** forms.

Underline the adverb that correctly completes each sentence.

1. Josh (thoughtfully   more thoughtfully) brought Helena some ice for her wounded knee.
2. My brother accepted the apology (graciously   more graciously) than I had expected.
3. Our wood stove heats the house (more efficiently   most efficiently) than the electric heater.
4. The (earlier   earliest) showing of the movie is at 11:30 a.m.
5. Winter seemed to arrive (sooner   soonest) than expected this year.

Complete the chart by writing the missing forms of each adverb.

POSITIVE	COMPARATIVE	SUPERLATIVE
6. _____	_____	latest
7. _____	better	_____
8. happily	_____	_____
9. _____	worse	_____
10. _____	more/less fluently	_____
11. much	_____	_____
12. _____	_____	longest
13. little	_____	_____

Complete each sentence with an adverb from the chart above and the form indicated in parentheses.

14. History is the subject I like _____. (superlative)
15. Dana did _____ on this test than on the last one. (comparative)
16. Margie slept _____ of all the campers. (superlative)
17. He volunteered _____ than Pedro did. (comparative)
18. I _____ accepted the job of stage manager. (positive)
19. The new student reads this difficult text _____ than I can. (comparative)

For additional help, review pages 114–115 in your textbook or visit www.voyagesinenglish.com.

Section 6 • 73

6.4 Troublesome Words

Troublesome adverbs are those adverbs that are commonly confused and often incorrectly used. When you use these adverbs in your writing, slow down and check that you are using the correct adverb.

Underline the correct adverb in parentheses to complete each sentence.

1. I found my name (further   farther) down the list.

2. (There   They're) ready to ship the packages tomorrow.

3. After so much training, Liz draws really (well   good).

4. Her paintings are (well   good).

5. I feel (bad   badly) about not studying for the spelling test.

6. Will you be going to (there   their) garage sale?

7. Alma gets along (well   good) with her brother.

8. The old carpet was (bad   badly) worn in several spots.

9. The family will go (they're   there) at the end of the vacation.

10. If you want an apple, here is a (well   good) one.

11. Do you have (they're   their) CDs?

12. Both soccer teams played (well   good).

13. We researched the issue (farther   further) before voting on it.

14. Mom was upset that the baby behaved (bad   badly) during the show.

Complete each sentence with *there, their,* or *they're*.

15. Max, Malachi, and Jacob are packing _____ things for a camping trip.

16. _____ going to Seven Mountains with the scouts.

17. Max says he loves to go _____ even though _____ are bears.

18. _____ black bears that are searching for food.

19. The scouts are very careful not to leave food out _____.

20. Malachi and Jacob are bringing _____ compasses.

21. _____ hoping to earn an orienteering merit badge.

22. _____ enthusiasm is growing for the camping trip.

23. _____ is always an adventure waiting for them at Seven Mountains.

© Loyola Press. Voyages in English   Grade 7

For additional help, review pages 116–117 in your textbook or visit www.voyagesinenglish.com.

6.4 Troublesome Words

> **Troublesome adverbs** are those adverbs that are commonly confused and often incorrectly used. When you use these adverbs in your writing, slow down and check that you are using the correct adverb.

Complete each sentence with _farther_ or _further_.

1. With the binoculars we could see _____ than before.

2. We had to walk _____ than we wanted.

3. We agreed there was nothing _____ to say on the subject.

4. Is it _____ to the state of Washington or to Washington, D.C., from here?

5. This strange concept could not be _____ from the truth.

Complete each sentence with _good_ or _well_.

6. We wanted to see _____ examples of modern art, so we went to the museum.

7. The twins behaved _____ at the dentist, so we all got to go to a movie.

8. Micah executes karate moves _____ because he has a black belt.

9. The entire class had _____ attendance, so we earned extra credit.

10. Eden explained _____ how to multiply fractions.

Complete each sentence with _bad_ or _badly_.

11. The music was discordant and _____ played.

12. I felt _____ about losing Sara's car keys.

13. Fuzzy was not a _____ dog; in fact, he was easy to train.

14. The food was _____, but the conversation was excellent.

15. The planning was thorough, but it was _____ executed.

Write a sentence using each word as an adverb.

16. farther _____

17. further _____

18. well _____

19. badly _____

20. there _____

For additional help, review pages 116–117 in your textbook or visit www.voyagesinenglish.com.

Section 6 • 75

6.5   Adverb Phrases and Clauses

Prepositional phrases used as adverbs to describe verbs, adjectives, or other adverbs are called **adverb phrases.** A dependent clause that acts as an adverb is called an **adverb clause.**

Underline each adverb phrase. Circle the word or words the phrase describes.

1. Many different ingredients complement each other in a recipe.
2. Holly contributes many ideas to the class.
3. Iron and carbon are forged together to form steel.
4. During the summer I earn money babysitting my younger brothers.
5. Julie uses nutmeg in casseroles, desserts, and even hot cocoa.

Underline each adverb clause. Circle the word or words the clause describes.

6. Until Henry needed to return home, he helped Mrs. McGillicuty.
7. The gyroscope stabilizes when it spins faster.
8. If there is a snowstorm tonight, school will be canceled.
9. While the children sing for the program, the group will perform a simple dance.
10. The spinning tires slip when they pass over the thin layer of ice.

Write an adverb phrase to complete the first sentence in each pair. Then write an adverb clause to complete the second sentence.

11. It snowed _____.

    It snowed _____.

12. The knight fought the dragon _____.

    The knight fought the dragon _____.

13. We slept _____.

    We slept _____.

14. Paulo will paint _____.

    Paulo will paint _____.

15. Jen can skate faster _____.

    Jen can skate faster _____.

16. We left for the airport _____.

    We left for the airport _____.

For additional help, review pages 118–119 in your textbook or visit www.voyagesinenglish.com.

SECTION 7 Daily Maintenance

7.1 **The smiling graduates marched proudly across the stage.**
   1. Which word is a participial adjective?   _____
   2. Which word is an adverb?   _____
   3. Is it an adverb of time, manner, or place?   _____
   4. What is the adverb phrase?   _____
   5. Diagram the sentence on another sheet of paper.

7.2 **Linda's new job, working with rescue dogs, is very interesting.**
   1. What is the gerund phrase?   _____
   2. How does it function in the sentence?   _____
   3. Which word is an adverb?   _____
   4. Is it an adverb of degree, time, or affirmation? _____
   5. Diagram the sentence on another sheet of paper.

7.3 **Why did you choose to apply for the coaching position?**
   1. What is the infinitive phrase?   _____
   2. How does it function in the sentence?   _____
   3. Which word is an interrogative adverb?   _____
   4. Which word is a participial adjective?   _____
   5. Diagram the sentence on another sheet of paper.

7.4 **My sister Laura sings more beautifully than I.**
1. What is the adverb?
2. Is the adverb comparative or superlative?
3. How is the word *Laura* used in the sentence?
4. What is the person of the pronoun *I*?
5. Diagram the sentence on another sheet of paper.

7.5 **Domingo plays best after he practices with his piano teacher.**
1. Which word is an adverb?
2. What word does it describe?
3. Is the adverb comparative or superlative?
4. Which word is a proper noun?
5. Diagram the sentence on another sheet of paper.

7.6 **When I feel sad, I write songs and poems.**
1. What is the adverb clause?
2. Which word does it describe?
3. Which words are the direct objects?
4. Are the verbs regular or irregular?
5. Diagram the sentence on another sheet of paper.

7.1 Single and Multiword Prepositions

A **preposition** is a word that shows the relationship between a noun or a pronoun and some other word in a sentence.

Underline each prepositional phrase. Circle each preposition.

1. Many species of jellyfish are found throughout the world's oceans.

2. According to one source, jellyfish are also known as medusa.

3. The jellyfish that are common to most coastal waters are the scyphozoan jellyfish.

4. During the spring, the number of jellyfish increases in response to an increase in food.

5. Over the course of the summer, jellyfish remain plentiful.

6. Because of the decline in food sources, jellyfish numbers decline in the fall and winter.

7. Jellyfish function by means of a web of nerves; they have no brain.

8. Instead of lungs, they simply absorb oxygen from the water around them.

9. Jellyfish may move through the water with contractions and stretches, but many simply float with the current.

10. Young jellyfish are tiny polyps that attach to the sea bottom.

11. When they reach a couple of millimeters, they float off into the water.

12. Most jellyfish aren't dangerous, but people avoid them on account of their painful sting.

Complete each sentence with a single or multiword preposition.

13. My mother and I walked _____ the garden, looking for her missing earring.

14. The train sped _____ the tunnel, illuminating the old stone walls.

15. I plan to study French _____ Spanish, as long as they both fit in my schedule.

16. We packed the clothes _____ our new suitcases and hoped for the best.

17. The outdoor concert was canceled _____ the weather.

18. _____ my brother, we are supposed to meet at Joseph's house tonight.

19. _____ the water main break, the entire student body was sent home.

20. I decided to wear my old jeans _____ a pair of shorts.

21. _____ the brilliant sunshine, it was only 15 degrees that day.

On another sheet of paper, write three sentences that each use a preposition. Use at least one multiword preposition.

© Loyola Press. Voyages in English   Grade 7

For additional help, review pages 124–125 in your textbook or visit www.voyagesinenglish.com.

Section 7 • 79

7.2 Troublesome Prepositions

Troublesome prepositions are commonly misused. Carefully consider the meanings of troublesome prepositions to determine which one fits the context of your writing.

Underline the misused preposition in each sentence.

1. Mike did not want Julia to be angry at herself.

2. Beside Mike, Ernesto and I were also trying to cheer her up.

3. "Life is as if a race you can't ever win, but you can't stop running," said Julia.

4. "Forgive me if I differ from you," replied Ernie, "but I think life is full of hope."

5. "Sometimes between all those racers, nice guys finish first," submitted Mike.

6. "Some days are breezy and warm and the sun shines all day," I contributed, "like the day was made just to touch your heart."

7. "Choosing my best day from between those this month is not easy," Ernesto pointed out.

8. Mike sat besides me and said, "Sometimes you study hard for a test, and you ace it."

9. Julia smiled like she said, "OK, maybe you have a point. Sometimes the glass is half full."

10. "Even better," I said, pulling a water bottle off my backpack, "Sometimes the glass is full."

Circle the word or words in parentheses to complete each sentence.

11. The lions were (beside   besides) the giraffes at the zoo.

12. The editor divided the writing assignments (between   among) the five reporters.

13. I had enough money to buy this bicycle (off of   from) my uncle.

14. His parents (differ on   differ from) their approach to discipline.

15. Brittany was (angry with   angry at) her little brother.

16. Leon has his own business (beside   besides) his full-time job.

17. Choosing (among   between) the two desserts was very difficult.

18. Monique swam (like   as if) her life depended on it.

19. Who (beside   besides) the Hendersons are coming to dinner tomorrow night?

20. I kicked the ball (off of   from) where it rested on the grass.

21. The committee's job was to choose (among   between) the five nominees to pick a winner.

22. Lydia's ideas (differ on   differ from) mine when it comes to picking great movies.

23. I (differ from   differ with) my parents on how I should spend my savings.

For additional help, review pages 126–127 in your textbook or visit www.voyagesinenglish.com.

© Loyola Press. Voyages in English Grade 7

7.2 Troublesome Prepositions

Troublesome prepositions are commonly misused. Carefully consider the meanings of troublesome prepositions in order to determine which one fits the context of your writing.

Complete each sentence with the correct preposition. Use each preposition once.

among	angry at	angry with	as	as if	beside	besides
between	differ with	differ on	differ from	from	like	off

1. Many people _____ the topic of wolves and other similar predators.

2. _____ wild animals, a great deal of research has been done on wolves.

3. If a wolf is _____ another wolf, it may arch its back and reveal its teeth.

4. _____ a heavy top coat, wolves have an undercoat of guard hairs.

5. There are common genetic traits _____ timber wolves and domestic dogs.

6. However, wolves _____ domesticated dogs in many important ways.

7. Wolves have large paws with webbing between the toes, and this trait gives wolves an advantage _____ predators.

8. Male and female wolves live together and do many activities _____ each other.

9. They may separate _____ each other to hunt prey.

10. A playful wolf may wag its tail _____ a domesticated dog.

11. The pack will dine _____ a single animal carcass.

12. A tense wolf may crouch _____ it is ready to pounce.

13. Some are _____ those who have improved the number of wolves in the wild.

14. Scientists may _____ ranchers on the importance of the wolf population.

Rewrite each sentence to correct errors in the use of prepositions.

15. We had to remove the trash off of the area around the stadium.

_____

16. The dog looked like no one had cared for it for months.

_____

For additional help, review pages 126–127 in your textbook or visit www.voyagesinenglish.com.

Section 7 • 81

7.3 Words Used as Adverbs and Prepositions

Some words can be either adverbs or prepositions. To distinguish between prepositions and adverbs, remember that a preposition must have an object.

Write whether each underlined word is used as an adverb (*A*) or a preposition (*P*).

1. Kioshi called out that he would see us <u>around</u>. _____
2. Can you see the clipper ship just <u>above</u> the horizon? _____
3. We walked <u>around</u> the block twice before finding the parakeet. _____
4. Jean fell <u>down</u> three times during the skating competition. _____
5. The ball went <u>through</u> the open window and landed on a couch. _____
6. The recovery crew is standing <u>by</u> for every football game. _____
7. Marcus and Caleb like to lead canoe trips <u>down</u> the river. _____
8. Please be home <u>before</u> supper to set the table. _____
9. <u>Below</u> the surface there is an abundance of minerals. _____
10. We needed to let the carpet dry <u>out</u> for a few days. _____

The first sentence in each pair uses the italicized word as an adverb. Add words to the second sentence to use the same word as a preposition.

11. Lift the box *off*. Lift the box *off* _____.
12. The squirrel scurried *along*. The squirrel scurried *along* _____.
13. I read this book *before*. I read this book *before* _____.
14. The wild mustang ran *near*. The wild mustang ran *near* _____.

Write two sentences for each word. Use the word as an adverb in the first sentence and as a preposition in the second sentence.

15. inside _____

     _____

16. around _____

     _____

17. since _____

     _____

For additional help, review pages 128–129 in your textbook or visit www.voyagesinenglish.com.

7.4 Prepositional Phrases as Adjectives

A propositional phrase that describes a noun or a pronoun is called an **adjective phrase**.

Underline the adjective phrase in each sentence. Circle the noun it describes.

1. The hometown of Melinda and Paul's family is Plainview.
2. McKenzie likes to write stories about fanciful creatures that talk.
3. We all thought the best plan for the club was to meet on Tuesday nights.
4. During the boycott we all refused to buy products from that store.
5. We all gasped when the sound of breaking dishes filled the air.
6. Several of the players hit home runs in today's game.
7. Each week she hopes she has chosen the winning numbers on a lottery ticket.
8. The balance of his checkbook was appallingly low.
9. The mesmerizing sound of this classical music makes me feel so relaxed.
10. The loose papers on the student's desk will be corrected after school.
11. The air is crisp and clear that first hour after sunrise.
12. Our family's annual trip to the beach was rather eventful.

Complete each sentence with an adjective phrase. Then circle the word that the adjective phrase describes.

13. The kitten _____ is stuck in the tree.
14. A person _____ shouted frantically for help.
15. Anne's photograph _____ won first prize in the contest.
16. Sarah enthusiastically enjoys reading books _____.
17. The colorful posters _____ are part of a class project.
18. Her child likes the ball _____.
19. The bride _____ held a bouquet of white roses.

Write a sentence for each noun. Include an adjective phrase to describe the noun.

20. roller coaster _____
21. basketball _____
22. passageway _____

For additional help, review pages 130–131 in your textbook or visit www.voyagesinenglish.com.

Section 7 • 83

7.5 Prepositional Phrases as Adverbs

Prepositional phrases that describe verbs, adjectives, or other adverbs are **adverb phrases.**

Underline the adverb phrases in these sentences. Circle the word each adverb phrase describes.

1. Her explanation seemed contrary to the facts.
2. The Board of Trustees meeting started at seven o'clock.
3. Our school closed during the summer, but some schools are open all year.
4. This spring's field trip was exciting for the students.
5. The pioneer family settled in Montana where its descendents are still found today.
6. We quietly watched the mouse creep farther into the hole.
7. Shane safely drove his new truck through the storm.
8. Stephen studied long hours about Egyptian pyramids.
9. The vehicle passed through the tollbooth and drove onto the bridge.
10. Chelsea plunged into the cold water but was protected by the special wet suit.
11. The raft landed on an island, and we were then disappointed that the ride was over.
12. The actors rehearsed on Saturday, but they did not meet on Sunday.

Complete each sentence with an adverb phrase. Then circle the word that the adverb phrase describes.

13. After the drill the students returned _____.
14. The president spoke late _____.
15. Before the show I felt nervous _____.
16. As they grow, tadpoles develop _____.
17. The Mendozas will begin _____.
18. Soon we will travel _____.
19. All the students emerge _____.
20. Our drama department needs props _____.
21. That cloud is shaped _____.
22. Those chickens lay eggs _____.
23. My cousin sets the fork _____.

For additional help, review pages 132–133 in your textbook or visit www.voyagesinenglish.com.

7.6 Prepositional Phrases as Nouns

Occasionally, a prepositional phrase is used as a noun. The prepositional phrase may act as a subject or as a subject complement.

Underline the prepositional phrase used as a noun in each sentence. Write whether the prepositional phrase functions as a *subject* or a *subject complement*.

1. In a hammock is a good place to read a book.   _____

2. The worst time to travel is in the winter.   _____

3. Before dinner is the best time to visit.   _____

4. Between June and August can be the warmest time of year.   _____

5. The way we usually travel is by passenger train.   _____

6. After school is the only time I can rehearse my music.   _____

7. A great swimming hole is near the waterfall.   _____

8. In the Bahamas is where I want to be.   _____

9. On the dresser was the place where she put her wallet.   _____

10. The conference that Mark attends is usually in March.   _____

11. A bad place to sing is at the library.   _____

12. Beside the heater might be a grand place to sit.   _____

Complete each sentence with a prepositional phrase used as a noun.

13. _____ was the best place to swim.

14. The young child was _____.

15. My least favorite place is _____.

16. _____ is where I keep a jar of change.

17. _____ will be considered out-of-bounds.

18. The usual place for the keys is _____.

19. The dog's typical position can be _____.

20. _____ is a method of transportation.

21. _____ was how she wore the necklace.

22. The lazy cat must be _____.

23. _____ is a great time to do homework.

24. The missing book was not _____.

For additional help, review pages 134–135 in your textbook or visit www.voyagesinenglish.com.

Section 7 • 85

SECTION 8   Daily Maintenance

8.1 **The photograph on this wall shows an image of Niagara Falls.**
1. What are the prepositions in the sentence?   _____
2. What are the prepositional phrases?   _____
3. Do they function as adverbs or adjectives?   _____
4. Which words do they describe?   _____
5. Diagram the sentence on another sheet of paper.

8.2 **Because of her hard work, Lucy raised her grade in math.**
1. What is the simple subject in the sentence?   _____
2. What is the single-word preposition?   _____
3. What is the multiword preposition?   _____
4. Which prepositional phrase describes *raised*?   _____
5. Diagram the sentence on another sheet of paper.

8.3 **Adrienne and I quietly walked past the sleeping baby.**
1. What is the simple subject in the sentence?   _____
2. Is *quietly* an adverb of degree, place, or manner?   _____
3. Is *past* used as an adverb or a preposition?   _____
4. Which word is a participial adjective?   _____
5. Diagram the sentence on another sheet of paper.

8.4 **The author of this novel also wrote a nonfiction book about Egypt.**
1. What are the prepositions in the sentence?   _____
2. What are the prepositional phrases?   _____
3. Which words do they describe?   _____
4. Is the word *also* an adjective or an adverb?   _____
5. Diagram the sentence on another sheet of paper.

8.5 **The mountain climbers watched in awe as an eagle flew above.**
   1. What is the complete subject in the sentence?   _____
   2. What is the dependent clause?   _____
   3. Is *above* used as a preposition or an adverb?   _____
   4. Which word does *above* describe?   _____
   5. Diagram the sentence on another sheet of paper.

8.6 **Some of my friends have eaten at this restaurant before.**
   1. What is the adjective phrase in the sentence?   _____
   2. Which word does the adjective phrase describe?   _____
   3. What is the tense of the verb?   _____
   4. Is *before* used as a preposition or an adverb?   _____
   5. Diagram the sentence on another sheet of paper.

8.7 **We arrived at the hotel late in the evening.**
   1. What is the simple subject and simple predicate?   _____
   2. Is *at the hotel* used as an adverb or adjective?   _____
   3. What word does it describe?   _____
   4. Is *late* used as an adjective or adverb?   _____
   5. Diagram the sentence on another sheet of paper.

8.8 **The ski trail on the left is perfect for beginners.**
   1. Which prepositional phrase acts as an adverb?   _____
   2. Which word does it describe?   _____
   3. How is *perfect* used in the sentence?   _____
   4. Which prepositional phrase describes *trail*?   _____
   5. Diagram the sentence on another sheet of paper.

8.9 **These red roses are beautiful, but I will buy those pink tulips.**
  1. What are the demonstrative adjectives?   _____
  2. What are the descriptive adjectives?   _____
  3. Which word is a linking verb?   _____
  4. Which noun and adjective does it link?   _____
  5. Diagram the sentence on another sheet of paper.

8.10 **Chelsea will wrap the gift while I look for some ribbon.**
  1. What is the adverb clause in the sentence?   _____
  2. What is the subordinate conjunction?   _____
  3. Which words does the adverb clause modify?   _____
  4. What type of adjective is the word *some*?   _____
  5. Diagram the sentence on another sheet of paper.

8.11 **At the beach is my favorite place.**
  1. What is the prepositional phrase?   _____
  2. What is the complete subject?   _____
  3. What is the subject complement?   _____
  4. What type of adjective is the word *my*?   _____
  5. Diagram the sentence on another sheet of paper.

© Loyola Press. Voyages in English **Grade 7**

8.1 Kinds of Sentences

A **sentence** is a group of words that expresses a complete thought. A sentence consists of a complete subject and a complete predicate. Sentences can be declarative, interrogative, imperative, and exclamatory.

Underline each complete subject once and each complete predicate twice.

1. Alfred Sisley was a French painter in the Impressionist tradition.
2. His English parents supported him during the years of his youth.
3. After the war his family lost everything.
4. Did you know that Sisley's work did not immediately receive recognition?
5. You should see this artist's beautiful work.
6. Sisley's paintings are especially famous for their accurate portrayal of the French countryside.
7. The images of the intense blue skies help me imagine myself in France.
8. Who would not want to be able to paint like that?

Rewrite each declarative sentence as an imperative sentence, an interrogative sentence, and an exclamatory sentence. Add or delete words as needed.

9. The boys are going to plan a picnic.

   Imperative: _____

   Interrogative: _____

   Exclamatory: _____

10. I want you to think about the opportunities.

    Imperative: _____

    Interrogative: _____

    Exclamatory: _____

11. Our homeroom teacher will assign jobs to everyone.

    Imperative: _____

    Interrogative: _____

    Exclamatory: _____

12. It is important to work together on this project.

    Imperative: _____

    Interrogative: _____

    Exclamatory: _____

For additional help, review pages 140–141 in your textbook or visit www.voyagesinenglish.com.

Name_____ Date_____

8.2 Adjective and Adverb Phrases

A **phrase** is a group of words that is used as a single part of speech. A phrase can be prepositional, participial, or infinitive. A phrase often functions as an adjective or an adverb.

Write *PREP* (prepositional), *PART* (participial), or *INF* (infinitive) to identify the italicized phrase in each sentence. Then write *ADV* (adverb) or *ADJ* (adjective) to identify how the phrase is used.

	TYPE OF PHRASE	USED AS
1. Weston remarked that he had never traveled *on a train*.	_____	_____
2. *Telling a happy story*, the speaker laughed.	_____	_____
3. Holt Skating Rink *in the park* was closed today.	_____	_____
4. Allison's bouquet *of flowers* looked beautiful.	_____	_____
5. People came *to see the movie star*.	_____	_____
6. *Feeling tired*, the small child took a nap.	_____	_____
7. Lee looked *in the attic* to find the old trunk.	_____	_____
8. A good time *to get bread* is in the morning.	_____	_____
9. *Running in circles*, the children sang and laughed.	_____	_____
10. Each show ends *with a fireworks display*.	_____	_____

Underline each adjective phrase once and each adverb phrase twice. Write whether each phrase is prepositional (*PREP*), participial (*PART*), or infinitive (*INF*).

11. "Russian mountains" were frozen water over tall wood structures. _____

12. The mountains were built during the 17th and 18th centuries. _____

13. No one knows where the idea to build them originated. _____

14. Rising as high as 80 feet in the air, the mountains were a formidable sight. _____

15. People rode down the ice mountains on sleds. _____

16. The mountains inspired rides in other parts of Europe. _____

17. Using sleds on wheels, these rides predated the modern roller coaster. _____

18. Roller coasters are a special kind of rail system. _____

19. The first roller coaster patent was issued on January 20, 1885. _____

20. Roller coasters have tracks that rise and fall in elevation. _____

21. Flipping the rider upside down, some designs have inversions. _____

22. Most modern roller coasters are found in amusement parks. _____

23. Roller coaster designers want to produce an exciting sensation. _____

© Loyola Press. Voyages in English Grade 7

For additional help, review pages 142–143 in your textbook or visit www.voyagesinenglish.com.

90 • Section 8

8.3 Adjective Clauses

A **clause** is a group of words that has a subject and a predicate. An independent clause is one that expresses a complete thought and so can stand on its own. A dependent clause cannot stand on its own.

Underline the adjective clause in each sentence. Circle the noun that each adjective clause describes.

1. This bus, which is at our stop, will be going downtown.

2. This is the movie that I told you about.

3. England is the place where the story begins.

4. My sister, whom I took ice-skating, enjoyed her day.

5. That author, whose books are popular with children, will be at our library.

6. Mr. Vogel, who is my favorite teacher, is going on vacation.

7. Spring is the time when birds build their nests.

8. Dominique is the reason why I joined the photography club.

9. Canada is ruled by a constitutional monarch, who is known as the Queen of Canada.

10. Lincoln School, which usually holds its Sports Day in June, is moving the event to May.

11. Carrots, which are easy to grow yourself, are rich in key vitamins.

12. The most surprising feature of the new car, which runs on electricity, is its low cost.

Underline the adjective clause in each sentence. Circle the relative pronoun or subordinate conjunction in the adjective clause.

13. The praying mantis, which is primarily diurnal, relies heavily on its sense of sight.

14. Insects that the praying mantis eats include some agricultural pests.

15. The praying mantis's head, which can turn almost 300 degrees, is heart-shaped.

16. When it spies its victim, the praying mantis grabs and holds its live prey.

Write an adjective clause to complete each sentence.

17. This morning, _____, I barely made it to school on time.

18. First, there was the incident with the peanut butter _____.

19. Then my brother, _____, couldn't find his trumpet.

20. Next, my mother couldn't find her keys _____.

21. My hope _____ was seeming pretty far-fetched.

22. We found the trumpet and keys and ran out to the car _____.

For additional help, review pages 144–145 in your textbook or visit www.voyagesinenglish.com.

8.4 Restrictive and Nonrestrictive Clauses

Restrictive clauses are essential clauses without which a sentence will not make sense. An adjective clause that is not essential to the meaning of a sentence is a **nonrestrictive clause.**

Write if the italicized adjective clause is restrictive (R) or nonrestrictive (N).

1. Ancient Greek theater, *which was well-developed by 5th century BC,* was very different from attending a modern play. _____

2. The three men *who were the actors* played all the roles. _____

3. The venue, *which was always an outdoor theater,* was a large half-circle. _____

4. The plays *that were produced* were only performed once. _____

5. Every play, *which was part of a religious festival,* honored Dionysus. _____

6. The polis, *who were the citizens of Greece,* paid for the production. _____

7. The plays, *which were highly structured,* competed with other plays for first, second, or third prize. _____

Underline each restrictive adjective clause once and each nonrestrictive adjective clause twice. Circle the noun to which each adjective clause refers.

8. Kabuki, which is a highly stylized form of Japanese theater, began in the early 17th century.

9. The Kabuki stage, which has special features and machinery, includes a hanamichi, or projection into the audience.

10. Chunori, which adds dramatic effect, lifts an actor into the air.

11. The wires that lift an actor into the air have been in use since the mid-19th century.

12. Seri are a series of stage traps, which raise and lower sets and actors on the stage.

13. The sets that rotate to make scene changes easier are called mawar-butai.

14. These special stage features, which were developed to make sudden plot revelations or character transformations possible, give Kabuki sophistication.

15. A Kabuki play that retells famous moments in Japanese history might go on for a full day.

16. A full-length play is done in five acts, which are each progressively faster in pace.

17. The final act, which should provide a satisfying resolution, is almost always very short.

18. Kabuki actors wear makeup that tells the audience something about their characters.

19. Kabuki actors who are well-known by the audience may be rewarded by having members of the audience call out their names or those of their fathers.

For additional help, review pages 146–147 in your textbook or visit www.voyagesinenglish.com.

8.4 Restrictive and Nonrestrictive Clauses

Restrictive clauses are essential clauses without which a sentence will not make sense. An adjective clause that is not essential to the meaning of a sentence is a **nonrestrictive clause.**

Choose and write an adjective clause to complete each sentence. Add commas as needed. Write if the clause is restrictive (R) or nonrestrictive (NR).

whose dog ran away	which grow in ponds and lakes
whose loom I bought	that I just finished reading
that was auctioned	which is famous for cheese production

1. The ball _____ was signed by Michael Jordan. _____

2. Water lilies _____ live on the surface of water. _____

3. The weaver _____ moved to Minnesota. _____

4. Tyrone is the neighbor _____. _____

5. Wisconsin _____
   is the country's largest producer of cranberries. _____

6. The biography _____ is excellent. _____

Write a restrictive or nonrestrictive adjective clause to complete each sentence. Add commas where necessary.

7. The pond _____ was stocked with fish.

8. My best friend _____ helped me.

9. Before tomorrow's concert _____ we will be ready.

10. The next game _____ is Friday.

11. The lens _____ captures special memories.

12. The rain _____ canceled our plans.

13. We saw the rainbow _____.

14. Our goal _____ was a worthy one.

15. We cleaned the table _____.

16. The new puppy _____ made us laugh.

For additional help, review pages 146–147 in your textbook or visit www.voyagesinenglish.com.

© Loyola Press. Voyages in English Grade 7

Section 8 • 93

8.5 Adverb Clauses

An **adverb clause** is a dependent clause used as an adverb. An adverb clause describes or gives information about a verb, an adjective, or an adverb.

Underline the adverb clause in each sentence. Circle the subordinate conjunction.

1. When it is summer in the Northern Hemisphere, it is winter in the Southern Hemisphere.
2. After the time ran out on the clock, the students cheered wildly.
3. Eric will peel the potatoes while we make the salad.
4. Gina wrapped all the presents before she went to bed.
5. Jack cupped his hands around his ears because he couldn't hear the speech.
6. Don't start the test until I give the signal.
7. We smelled the peach cobbler as soon as we entered the restaurant.
8. When I heard the phone ring, I ran into the kitchen to answer it.
9. Although the children were tired, they didn't want to go to bed.

Underline the adverb clause in each sentence. Circle the word or words each adverb clause modifies.

10. As long as the dogs are trained, they can participate in agility competitions.
11. If you and I help, others will volunteer their time too.
12. Since the Parkers like board games so much, they made every Monday game night.
13. During the holiday celebrations, few people worked unless the job was really necessary.
14. When the beverages arrived, we added them to the buffet table.
15. After I clean my room, I plan to play soccer with my friends.
16. The class sang silly songs on the bus wherever we went on the field trip.
17. John wasn't interested in math until he was invited to compete in the contest.

Write an adverb clause to complete each sentence.

18. _____, I plan to attend the party.
19. _____, she usually swims well.
20. The batter has hit the ball harder _____.
21. I often write best _____.
22. _____, Jake will not be able to join you.

For additional help, review pages 148–149 in your textbook or visit www.voyagesinenglish.com.

8.6 Noun Clauses as Subjects

Dependent clauses can be used as nouns. These clauses, called **noun clauses,** typically begin with introductory words such as *how, that, what, whatever, when, where, whether, who, whoever, whom, whomever,* and *why.*

Underline the noun clause used as a subject in each sentence.

1. That my brother can climb the fence amazes me.
2. Whatever ate the apple is still in the yard.
3. Whoever arrived last left the door wide open.
4. Whomever we pick should already be a member of the club.
5. Why we keep losing the key to the back door is a mystery to me.
6. How this puzzle goes together is bewildering us.
7. What the principal had in mind was a celebration in the multipurpose room.
8. Whoever saw our dog in the field said he still had his collar on.
9. What Mr. Alexander did was teach us all a new way to do long division.
10. When we plan to go to the store determines whether there is time for one more game.
11. Whether Joe had wanted to quit the team was forgotten after his winning season.
12. Where the dog escaped the yard was a puzzle until we found the hole in the fence.

Choose an introductory word to complete each noun clause. Then underline the entire noun clause that is used as a subject.

13. _____ they are going is unknown.
14. _____ the girls did with the treasure is a secret.
15. _____ you want for dessert is fine with me.
16. _____ Joe should feel this way came as a surprise to all of us.
17. _____ no one remembered the homework assignment was hard to explain.
18. _____ the magician made the tiger disappear was all we talked about.
19. _____ has worked at the pool will come back again.
20. _____ they want to visit their parents will be decided later.
21. _____ we ask should already have experience with a hockey stick.
22. _____ owns this book is unclear, but there are ways to find out.
23. _____ he will be arriving is written on the itinerary.

For additional help, review pages 150–151 in your textbook or visit www.voyagesinenglish.com.

Section 8 • 95

8.7 Noun Clauses as Subject Complements

Like nouns, noun clauses can be used as subject complements.

Underline the noun clause used as a subject complement in each sentence. Circle the subject that the noun clause describes or renames.

1. Michael's greatest achievement was that he earned a scholarship at the technology fair.

2. The question is whether or not Mrs. Holcolmb can drive us all to the game tomorrow.

3. One theory explaining the disappearance of the cake is that the dog ate it.

4. Another suggestion has been that we all go together in one van to save on gas.

5. Something to think about is how we are going to get everyone to the competition.

6. A reason for concern is whether or not it might snow tonight.

Underline the noun clause in each sentence. Indicate if the noun clause is used as a subject (_S_) or as a subject complement (_SC_).

7. What I had for breakfast made me feel better. _____

8. Her wish was that all her friends could come to the party. _____

9. The truth was that Mary was faster than Ted. _____

10. Whatever the teacher said was inspiring. _____

11. Our main concern at the moment was how to get home before dark. _____

12. The problem was that I forgot my homework. _____

13. Jay's goal is that he can buy a new amplifier. _____

14. What role he played is still a puzzle to the committee. _____

15. That he would win the contest was taken for granted. _____

16. The second house from the corner is where the Jacobs live. _____

17. One of the school's mysteries is what is behind the locked red door. _____

18. The fact is that February is a good month for ice-skating. _____

Write a noun clause used as a subject complement to complete each sentence.

19. Randall's best character trait was _____.

20. Mrs. Smith's favorite lesson is _____.

21. The best prize is _____.

22. My hope for the future is _____.

© Loyola Press. Voyages in English   Grade 7

For additional help, review pages 152–153 in your textbook or visit www.voyagesinenglish.com.

8.8 Noun Clauses as Appositives

A noun clause can be used as an appositive. An appositive follows a noun and renames it or gives more information about it.

Underline the noun clause used as an appositive in each sentence.

1. The fact that the store doesn't open until noon prevented us from going any earlier.
2. Many accepted the idea that the club could not function without a secretary.
3. Despite their belief that if they didn't wear their lucky shirts their team would lose, they opted to wear the new uniforms.
4. The understanding that the understudy would get to perform in one show encouraged Carol.
5. Mom wrote out her request that Mr. Oz should assign more math homework in a note.
6. Dad is a fan of the principle that the Super Bowl is an unofficial national holiday.

Underline the clause used as an appositive in each sentence. Then write whether it is a *noun clause* or an *adjective clause.*

7. Marie's hope that she would become a doctor came true. _____
8. All the flowers that I planted last month are in bloom. _____
9. Jack asked the question whether the campers should leave in the morning. _____
10. The report, whatever it was, caused the soldiers to celebrate. _____
11. It is a fact that our club sold the most raffle tickets. _____
12. The fact that exercise promotes good health is obvious. _____
13. The Persian rugs that are in the storeroom will go in the hall. _____
14. She voiced her concern that it would be dark soon. _____
15. The man's announcement that he had the winning lottery ticket thrilled his wife. _____
16. Some of the pictures that I took during my trip are in this album. _____

Write a sentence that uses each noun clause as an appositive.

17. that animals act strangely before an earthquake _____

_____

18. whether we should cancel due to rain _____

_____

For additional help, review pages 154–155 in your textbook or visit www.voyagesinenglish.com.

8.9   Noun Clauses as Direct Objects

A noun clause can act as a direct object. The introductory word *that* is often dropped from a noun clause used as a direct object, but omitting *that* after the verbs *feel, learn, say, see,* or *think* may change the meaning of a sentence.

Underline the direct object in each sentence. Identify whether it is a noun (*N*) or a noun clause (*NC*).

1. I'll choose whichever car gets the best gas mileage.   _____

2. She wondered what might be inside the box.   _____

3. Dad suggested that we help him set up the tent.   _____

4. The children sent letters to their pen pals.   _____

5. We discussed how we wanted to spend the money.   _____

6. Joshua asked Sofia for help with dinner preparations.   _____

Use the information about the speaker to write a noun clause used as a direct object to complete each sentence.

7. a young child

   "I hate _____."

8. a college student

   "I must decide _____."

9. a police officer

   "I explained _____."

10. a coach

    "I hope _____."

11. a salesperson

    "I believe _____."

12. a ship's captain

    "I decided _____."

13. a teenager

    "I understand _____."

14. a teacher

    "I require _____."

For additional help, review pages 156–157 in your textbook or visit www.voyagesinenglish.com.

8.10 Noun Clauses as Objects of Prepositions

A noun clause can function as the object of a preposition. An adjective clause is sometimes confused with a noun clause used as an object of a preposition. An adjective clause describes a noun or pronoun in the independent clause.

Underline the noun clause used as an object of a preposition.

1. The girls were thinking about what they could do to win Saturday's softball game.
2. I searched on the Internet for what other schools were doing to raise library funds.
3. This week we learned about how apple crisp is made.
4. What was the purpose of what those people were doing?
5. The principal must agree to whatever the clubs propose for activities.

Underline the noun clause in each sentence. Write whether each noun clause is the _subject_, the _direct object_, or the _object of a preposition_.

6. The doctor gives advice to whoever will listen.   _____
7. That I was angry must have been noticed by many people.   _____
8. Liz read about what should be planted here.   _____
9. I was amazed by what the baby could do.   _____
10. Whoever is chosen can participate in the event.   _____
11. Sam thinks that the horse is too young to ride.   _____
12. We wondered whether our money would be refunded.   _____
13. The host announced that the show would begin shortly.   _____
14. Whatever we decide will be noted in the minutes.   _____
15. Mei Ling was interested in what she heard about the movie.   _____

Write a noun clause used as an object of a preposition to complete each sentence.

16. The students learned about _____.
17. Our coach was astonished by _____.
18. Their next discussion focuses on _____.
19. Let's develop a plan for _____.
20. The reward will go to _____.

8.11 Simple, Compound, and Complex Sentences

A **simple sentence** is an independent clause that stands alone. A **compound sentence** contains two or more independent clauses. A **complex sentence** has one independent clause and at least one dependent clause.

Write *simple*, *compound*, or *complex* to identify the sentences in each set.

1. **a.** My friend invited me to a dance. I do not want to go.   _____

    b. My friend invited me to a dance, but I do not want to go.   _____

    c. Although my friend invited me to a dance, I do not want to go.   _____

2. **a.** Paul, who studies history, knows Elaine, who studies math.   _____

    b. Paul studies history. Elaine studies math.   _____

    c. Paul studies history, and Elaine studies math.   _____

3. **a.** The explorers were ready. They entered the submarine.   _____

    b. When the explorers were ready, they entered the submarine.   _____

    c. The explorers were ready, so they entered the submarine.   _____

Underline each independent clause once and each dependent clause twice. Circle the relative pronouns and subordinate conjunctions.

4. Robin of Loxley, who was also known as Robin Hood, was a mythical character.

5. Robin Hood is said to have been a contemporary of King Richard II, whom Robin supported.

6. The name most often refers to an individual, but it was also a name for any outlaw.

7. Those written references, which are initially quite brief, refer to long-told oral tales.

8. Maid Marian and Friar Tuck appear in the stories, which were told through May Day plays, at the end of the 15th century.

9. Robin Hood was a yeoman, so he was neither royalty nor a peasant.

10. The truth of Robin's story, which is hotly debated, certainly is entertaining.

Use the information in parentheses to write a clause to complete each sentence.

11. _____, who has been a great help to me.
    (independent clause)

12. I enjoy bicycling, _____. (independent clause with a coordinating conjunction).

13. I sang a song _____. (dependent clause)

14. Even though I don't like astronomy, _____.
    (independent clause)

For additional help, review pages 160–161 in your textbook or visit www.voyagesinenglish.com.

SECTION 9 Daily Maintenance

9.1 **The dress with pink flowers is beautiful, but I want this red skirt.**
   1. Is the sentence simple, compound, or complex? _____
   2. Is the sentence declarative or interrogative?   _____
   3. What is the adjective phrase?   _____
   4. Which word is a subject complement?   _____
   5. Diagram the sentence on another sheet of paper.

9.2 **Martha is wearing a sweater that her grandmother knitted.**
   1. Is the sentence declarative or imperative?   _____
   2. What is the adjective clause?   _____
   3. Which word does this clause describe?   _____
   4. What is the independent clause?   _____
   5. Diagram the sentence on another sheet of paper.

9.3 **Did you thank the man who found your purse?**
   1. Is the sentence imperative or interrogative?   _____
   2. What is the adjective clause?   _____
   3. Is this clause restrictive or nonrestrictive?   _____
   4. Which words are used as direct objects?   _____
   5. Diagram the sentence on another sheet of paper.

9.4 **If you need help in math, I can tutor you on weekends.**
1. Is the sentence simple, compound, or complex? _____
2. What is the subordinate conjunction? _____
3. What is the adverb clause? _____
4. Is this clause dependent or independent? _____
5. Diagram the sentence on another sheet of paper.

9.5 **That Meg is a talented artist is obvious.**
1. Is the sentence simple, compound, or complex? _____
2. What is the noun clause? _____
3. What is the introductory word of the clause? _____
4. What is the subject complement? _____
5. Diagram the sentence on another sheet of paper.

9.6 **We can only hope that he arrives before noon.**
1. What is the verb phrase in the sentence? _____
2. What is the noun clause? _____
3. What is the adverb phrase? _____
4. What does this phrase describe? _____
5. Diagram the sentence on another sheet of paper.

© Loyola Press. Voyages in English Grade 7

9.1 Coordinating Conjunctions

A **conjunction** is a word used to connect words or groups of words. A **coordinating conjunction** joins words or groups of words that are similar.

Underline the coordinating conjunction in each sentence.

1. Poodles and Portuguese water dogs love physical activity.

2. These breeds originated in Asia, but they were imported all over the world.

3. The Portuguese water dog would herd fish into nets and carry items from boat to boat.

4. Today the dogs are primarily good companions, yet they are still used in some professions.

5. The highly trainable and playful nature of the poodle make it a good performer.

6. The athletic and hard-working nature of the Portuguese water dog makes it a good water rescue dog.

7. Both dogs need careful grooming and a lot of exercise.

8. The poodle or the Portuguese water dog would make a great choice for a family pet.

Circle the coordinating conjunction in each sentence. Then write whether each conjunction joins *words*, *phrases*, or *clauses*.

9. Sam needs to practice every day, or he may not pass the test. _____

10. Brittany decided to study physics and chemistry. _____

11. The cat ran down the stairs and into the basement. _____

12. Stephanie writes to her cousins but calls her friends. _____

13. I will lend you money, but you must pay me back. _____

14. Nancy takes cream and sugar in her coffee. _____

15. She loves animals yet hesitates to keep a pet. _____

16. The author did not speak long, nor did he sign any books. _____

17. The police car raced down the street and into the alley. _____

18. He is small but strong. _____

Write three sentences with coordinating conjunctions. Connect two words in the first sentence, two phrases in the second, and two clauses in the third.

_____

_____

_____

_____

For additional help, review pages 166–167 in your textbook or visit www.voyagesinenglish.com.

9.2 Correlative Conjunctions

> **Correlative conjunctions** are conjunctions that are used in pairs to connect words or groups of words that have equal importance in a sentence.

Circle the correlative conjunctions. Not all sentences have correlative conjunctions.

1. Our neighbor's garden has both flowers and shrubbery.
2. The team won not only the district championship but also the state championship.
3. Neither my mother nor my sister has red hair.
4. For dinner we had the choice of either chicken or steak.
5. Robyn and Joanna are both ordering spaghetti for lunch.
6. Whether he is winning or losing, Jim is always upbeat and optimistic.
7. Will you bring potato salad or deviled eggs to the picnic?
8. Both Carl and Leslie will enter the pie-eating contest.
9. My mom not only cooked all the food but also made the decorations.
10. We can spend the day at either the river or the lake.

Write correlative conjunctions from the box to complete each sentence.

both . . . and	not only . . . but also	neither . . . nor
either . . . or	whether . . . or	

11. _____ squid _____ eel are considered edible.

12. I don't know _____ rain _____ snow is in the forecast.

13. _____ this chair _____ that one would fit around the table.

14. Football is _____ a game of strategy _____ physical fitness.

15. _____ can the seventh graders help, _____ they can _____ draw the posters to advertise the event.

16. _____ the library _____ the post office is open today.

17. _____ can Jake draw, _____ he can _____ sculpt.

18. I can't tell _____ I feel better _____ not.

19. _____ tacos _____ pizza would be a welcome treat for dinner.

20. _____ this book _____ that one is written in English.

© Loyola Press. Voyages in English   Grade 7

For additional help, review pages 168–169 in your textbook or visit www.voyagesinenglish.com.

9.3 Conjunctive Adverbs

Conjunctive adverbs connect independent clauses. A semicolon is used before the conjunctive adverb, and a comma is used after it. **Parenthetical expressions** are used in the same way as conjunctive adverbs.

Circle the correct conjunctive adverb or parenthetical expression to complete each sentence.

1. My brother plays golf at least once a week; (moreover   however), he often attends golfing classes on the weekend.

2. It was extremely foggy the day of the tour; (later   consequently), we were able to spot very few eagles.

3. I live in an area where groundhogs are common; (furthermore   nevertheless), the first time I saw one I thought it was a beaver.

4. There are many lakes in Minnesota; (in fact   nevertheless), the state's slogan is "Land of 10,000 Lakes."

5. Juanita isn't afraid of roller coasters; (otherwise   on the contrary), she was one of the first people to ride on the Cobra.

6. We have spent a long time on our homework; (finally   still), we can't solve the last two problems.

7. Gwen has always liked math and is very good at it; (however   therefore), she plans to become a math teacher.

8. Nate enjoys playing soccer and tennis; (besides   however), he has decided to try out for only one team.

9. Bob's Smoke Pit has great food; (indeed   therefore), it has the best ribs in town.

10. Our cabin is in the mountains; (however   therefore), we see many wild animals.

11. Danielle doesn't want to make a ceramic pot; (moreover   instead), she plans to make a large serving platter.

12. The waves are too high for surfing; (besides   consequently), the water is too cold.

Write a conjunctive adverb to complete each sentence.

13. Inventors are interested in things that make our lives easier; _____, many inventions are intended for use in the home.

14. Most dogs were working animals; _____, they were bred for specific jobs.

15. On the conductor's command, an orchestra may begin playing; _____, the musicians follow the conductor's signals for pace and volume.

16. Abby is getting good grades; _____, she wants to do even better.

For additional help, review pages 170–171 in your textbook or visit www.voyagesinenglish.com.

Section 9 • 105

9.4 Subordinate Conjunctions

A **subordinate conjunction** is used to join an independent clause and a dependent clause.

Underline the subordinate conjunction in each sentence.

1. Because the understudy knew her lines, the show was saved.
2. We brought two balls so that we would have a spare if one was lost.
3. If anyone hosted a party, the neighbors were sure to show up.
4. Elliot's talent was in baseball, while Adam's talent was in football.
5. John jumped around the room, waving his arms as if he were playing a guitar.

Circle the subordinate conjunction in each sentence.
Underline the dependent clause.

6. She acts as if nothing is wrong.
7. While they were in New York, it snowed 20 inches.
8. The basketball team forfeited the game because not enough players showed up.
9. We used bright colors so that our signs would stand out from the others.
10. Ellen has been driving to school since she turned 18.
11. I prefer tomatoes when they have ripened on the vine.
12. Trina skated better than she had ever skated before.
13. Why don't we wait here until it is time to leave?
14. After Chris heard about the accident, he rushed to the hospital.
15. When we visited Yosemite, we hiked to the top of Half Dome.
16. Although I like this dress, I cannot afford to buy it.
17. Kim will go to the concert even though she has not finished her homework.

Complete each sentence with an appropriate dependent clause beginning with a subordinate conjunction.

18. _____, they were ready to go to the movies.
19. _____, many people see a dentist twice a year.
20. _____, Julie did her homework every night.
21. _____, Ty grew to enjoy the talks with his aunt.
22. _____, you might be late for sports practice.
23. _____, the group decided to continue sledding.

For additional help, review pages 172–173 in your textbook or visit www.voyagesinenglish.com.

9.5   Troublesome Conjunctions

Some conjunctions are frequently misused or confused.

Write *without* or *unless* to complete each sentence.

1. _____ proper storage, the lawn mower may rust over the winter.

2. Don't pick up that book _____ you have the time to read the entire thing.

3. _____ we find a used part for the car, we won't be able to leave on our trip.

4. The animal will not thrive _____ sufficient food and water.

5. Buy three tickets for the show _____ your sister says she doesn't want to go.

6. _____ my brothers in the house, it is very quiet around here.

7. _____ more parents can attend, the field trip will have to be canceled.

Circle the correct item to complete each sentence.

8. (Unless   Without) his bus pass, he will not be able to ride the bus today.

9. I read through the magazine (as   like) I waited.

10. He acted (like   as if) he didn't get enough sleep.

11. Don't leave (unless   without) I call you first.

12. The huge snake looked (like   as if) a tree branch in the sand.

13. A computer won't work (unless   without) you plug it in.

14. (Unless   Without) the weather gets colder, we won't be able to go ice-skating.

15. I felt (like   as if) nothing could go wrong.

16. The climbers grew weary (like   as) the guide led them along the steep paths.

17. Our car looked (like   as if) no one had washed it in quite some time.

18. Gary ordered a sandwich (unless   without) onions or pickles.

19. The sound of the katydids in the trees was (like   as if) that of rain on the canopy.

Rewrite each sentence to correct the use of conjunctions and prepositions.

20. The dogs were barking like there was a stranger in the yard.

    _____

21. The birds made their nest in the old wasps' nest, like my friend told me.

    _____

22. You must see the new high school building it looks like a huge cement block.

    _____

9.6 Interjections

An **interjection** is a word that expresses a strong or sudden emotion.

Circle the interjection that is the best match for each sentence.

1. (Yikes   Yum), that had to hurt!
2. (Wow   No)! That last fireworks display was the best.
3. (Hello   Enough)! It's time to end the game and go inside.
4. (Sh   Oh, no)! The baby is finally asleep.
5. (Bravo!   Hush!) That was an excellent story for such a young author.
6. (Beware   Good grief), I really thought that she was going to steal second base!
7. (Gosh   Hooray)! I thought I had more money than this.
8. (Ha   Indeed)! That trick worked really well this time.
9. (Hush   Whew)! The bell will ring in just one more minute.

Write a sentence with an interjection to match each situation.

10. a server in a restaurant who just dropped a tray of food

    _____

11. a construction worker who hit his thumb with a hammer

    _____

12. a librarian quieting children

    _____

13. a scientist making an important discovery

    _____

14. a child tasting her favorite food

    _____

15. a person watching trapeze artists at a circus

    _____

16. a student who discovers that she has forgotten her homework

    _____

17. a customer politely seeking the attention of a salesclerk

    _____

For additional help, review pages 176–177 in your textbook or visit www.voyagesinenglish.com.

SECTION 10 Daily Maintenance

10.1 **A goldfish or a gerbil is a good pet for most children.**
1. Is the sentence or the subject compound? _____
2. What is the correlative conjunction? _____
3. Which word is a subject complement? _____
4. What is the adjective phrase? _____
5. Diagram the sentence on another sheet of paper.

10.2 **Silvia studied for the English test; however, she made several errors.**
1. Is the sentence simple, compound, or complex? _____
2. What is the conjunctive adverb? _____
3. What is the adverb phrase? _____
4. Which word is an indefinite adjective? _____
5. Diagram the sentence on another sheet of paper.

10.3 **When I lived in Canada, I often visited Lake Louise.**
1. Is the sentence simple, compound, or complex? _____
2. What is the subordinate conjunction? _____
3. What is the adverb clause? _____
4. Which word is an adverb? _____
5. Diagram the sentence on another sheet of paper.

10.4 **Liam cannot go unless his parents give their permission.**
1. Is the sentence simple, compound, or complex? _____
2. What is the subordinate conjunction? _____
3. What is the independent clause? _____
4. Which words are possessive adjectives? _____
5. Diagram the sentence on another sheet of paper.

10.5 **Wow! Lin's illustrations for this book look exquisite.**
1. What is the adjective phrase in the sentence? _____
2. What is the linking verb? _____
3. What is the subject complement? _____
4. What is the interjection? _____
5. Diagram the sentence on another sheet of paper.

10.1 Periods and Commas

> A **period** is used at the end of a declarative or an imperative sentence, after an abbreviation, and after the initials in a name. **Commas** are used in a variety of ways to separate or set off words, phrases, and clauses.

Add commas where needed in these sentences. Then write the letter of the comma rule used in each sentence.

A.	to separate words in a series	**E.**	to set off dates
B.	to set off nonrestrictive phrases and clauses	**F.**	to set off place names
C.	to set off words of direct address	**G.**	to set off divided quotations
D.	to set off parenthetical expressions		

1. "After you finish your homework" said Maria "I have a surprise for you."   _____

2. He was born in Fairbanks Alaska but he now lives in Seattle Washington.   _____

3. The package will be there I promise you by next Tuesday.   _____

4. Myra I can't make it to the play tonight.   _____

5. The Declaration of Independence was signed on July 4 1776.   _____

6. Ronald Reagan who had once been an actor became our 40th president.   _____

7. Theresa went to the grocery store and bought bread milk and cheese.   _____

Rewrite the sentences to correct any errors in punctuation.

8. I e-mailed Ms Emily Rayward, with my decision on Sept, 15.

_____

9. A local lawyer Mr Richard Kanton was quoted in the newspaper article yesterday

_____

10. Emma made an appointment with Dr Richardson for May 4. 2010

_____

11. Tussey Mountain near State College Penn is home to a small ski resort

_____

12. Yes Lilly, we do need to stop in Athens Georgia on the way home.

For additional help, review pages 182–183 in your textbook or visit www.voyagesinenglish.com.

Section 10 • 111

10.2 Exclamation Points, Question Marks, Semicolons, and Colons

Exclamation points are used after interjections and exclamatory sentences. **Question marks** are used to end interrogative sentences. **Semicolons** and **colons** are used in specific situations.

Add semicolons and colons where needed.

1. The singer used a microphone nevertheless, we couldn't hear him.
2. Dear Dr. Greenbaum
3. Sheila rides her bike to school I prefer to walk.
4. There was a blizzard last night hence, school was closed.
5. To Whom It May Concern
6. Please call these people Marvin, Jane, Anita, and Martha.
7. Joyce has three favorite hobbies namely, knitting, dancing, and rock climbing.
8. I will visit three countries this summer Greece, Spain, and Italy.

Add periods, question marks, or exclamation points where needed.

9. Hey, I can't believe you did that
10. Oh, no What kind of weather can we expect tomorrow
11. What is that strange lump I see in the snow
12. What interesting sights we can see through the Hubble Telescope
13. I decided to call everyone in my class for a party next Friday
14. Ah-ha I believe we have found the culprit who raided the cookie jar
15. Yikes Is that how far we have to run for the physical fitness test

Write a sentence for each topic. Use the correct punctuation.

16. a question about a vacation you would like to take

_____

17. an exclamation that shows happiness

_____

18. a question about your favorite subject

_____

19. an exclamation that is a warning

_____

© Loyola Press. Voyages in English   Grade 7

For additional help, review pages 184–185 in your textbook or visit www.voyagesinenglish.com.

10.3 Quotation Marks and Italics

Quotation marks are used with direct quotations. **Italics** are used for titles of books, magazines, newspapers, movies, TV series, and works of art and for the names of ships and aircraft.

Add quotation marks and other punctuation where needed. Use underlining to indicate italics.

1. Where can I park my bicycle asked Isaac.
2. Sylvia selected the short story called The Year that We Disappeared.
3. I am reading an article titled Budgeting for Teens in Family and Home Magazine.
4. No I'm sorry replied the clerk, but Watership Down is not currently in stock.
5. The boys left here just a half hour ago, said Mrs. Crosby.
6. Wow Look how high his paper airplane flew yelled Marcus.
7. I cannot find the book A Tree Grows in Brooklyn anywhere.
8. Becky suggested, We could all go to my house to practice for the play

Write a sentence for each topic. Include a title in your sentence. Underline words to indicate italics where needed.

9. your favorite movie

   _____

10. your favorite television show

   _____

11. your favorite book

   _____

12. your favorite magazine

   _____

13. a song that you like

   _____

14. a poem you have read

   _____

15. a magazine article you would like to write

   _____

For additional help, review pages 186–187 in your textbook or visit www.voyagesinenglish.com.

Section 10 • 113

10.4   Apostrophes, Hyphens, and Dashes

> **Apostrophes, hyphens,** and **dashes** are used to clarify text for the reader.

Circle the letter that correctly explains the punctuation mark that is needed in each sentence. Then add the punctuation mark to the sentence.

1. I turned my head it was only for a second and missed the final shot of the game.
   - **a.** A hyphen is used to separate parts of some compound words.
   - **b.** A dash is used to set off words that indicate a change in thought.

2. The mansion has twenty two rooms.
   - **a.** A hyphen is used in compound numbers between twenty-one and ninety-nine.
   - **b.** A dash is used to set off an appositive.

3. Sandy regularly borrows items from her sisters wardrobe.
   - **a.** An apostrophe shows possession.
   - **b.** An apostrophe is used to show the plurals of lowercase but not of capital letters, unless the plural could be mistaken for a word.

4. Call Raquel she's on the prom committee to get the directions.
   - **a.** A dash is used to set off an appositive that contains commas.
   - **b.** A dash is used to set off words that indicate a change in thought.

5. The *t*s were crossed, and the *i*s were dotted.
   - **a.** An apostrophe is used to show the plurals of lowercase but not of capital letters, unless the plural could be mistaken for a word.
   - **b.** An apostrophe shows possession.

Write a sentence for each description, using correct punctuation.

6. An apostrophe shows possession.

   _____

7. A dash is used to set off words that indicate a change in thought.

   _____

8. A hyphen is used in compound numbers between twenty-one and ninety-nine.

   _____

9. A hyphen is used to form some temporary adjectives.

   _____

For additional help, review pages 188–189 in your textbook or visit www.voyagesinenglish.com.

10.5 Capitalization

Using **capital letters** correctly provides valuable clues for the reader that make your writing easier to understand.

Use the proofreading symbol (≡) to show which letters should be capitalized.

1. my mother likes to watch old westerns.
2. usually, i won't watch them with her because i prefer more modern movies.
3. last week a huge snowstorm hit my town, plainview, minnesota.
4. alice, xander, and i went sledding, and my dad took me out on his snowmobile.
5. plainview isn't a very big town though, and everything was closed.
6. finally, i said, "i've been thinking, mom, that we should watch one of your movies."
7. she introduced me to john wayne and jack ely.
8. the towns all had names like dry gulch, deadwood, and windmill junction.
9. all in all, it wasn't a bad way to spend a day with my mother.

Write a sentence that illustrates each rule for using a capital letter.

10. a title when it precedes a person's name

_____

11. the first word in a sentence

_____

12. a direction when it refers to a part of the country

_____

13. an abbreviation of a word that is capitalized

_____

14. a proper noun

_____

15. a proper adjective

_____

16. the principal words in the title of a book, play, or poem

_____

17. the first word of a direct quotation

_____

For additional help, review pages 190–191 in your textbook or visit www.voyagesinenglish.com.

Section 10 • 115

SECTION 11 | Daily Maintenance

11.1 **Brandy served her father the largest piece of steak.**
1. How is the word *father* used in the sentence? _____
2. Is the verb regular or irregular? _____
3. What kind of adjective is the word *largest*? _____
4. How is the word *piece* used in the sentence? _____
5. Diagram the sentence on another sheet of paper.

11.2 **Stephen King, an author of many novels, is my favorite writer.**
1. What does the appositive rename? _____
2. Is the appositive restrictive or nonrestrictive? _____
3. Which noun is the object of a preposition? _____
4. How is the word *writer* used in the sentence? _____
5. Diagram the sentence on another sheet of paper.

11.3 **The students have studied weather, and now they will make a rain gauge.**
1. Is the sentence simple, compound, or complex? _____
2. Which word is a coordinating conjunction? _____
3. Which words are direct objects? _____
4. Which word is an adverb? _____
5. Diagram the sentence on another sheet of paper.

11.4 **The small birds collect blades of grass and weave them into nests.**
1. What is the complete subject? _____
2. Is the subject or the predicate compound? _____
3. What is the antecedent of the word *them*? _____
4. Which words are prepositions? _____
5. Diagram the sentence on another sheet of paper.

11.5 **Blowing in the wind, the dandelions are floating like snowflakes.**
1. What is the simple subject?   _____
2. What is the participial phrase?   _____
3. Does it act as an adjective or an adverb?   _____
4. What is the verb phrase?   _____
5. Diagram the sentence on another sheet of paper.

11.6 **I improved my tennis skills by taking lessons from my friend's coach.**
1. What kind of pronoun is the word *I*?   _____
2. Which word is a gerund?   _____
3. How is the gerund phrase used in the sentence? _____
4. Is the possessive noun singular or plural?   _____
5. Diagram the sentence on another sheet of paper.

11.7 **The raccoon is using its sharp claws to climb that tree.**
1. What is the infinitive phrase?   _____
2. Is it used as a direct object or an adverb?   _____
3. Is *its* a contraction or a possessive adjective? _____
4. What kind of adjective is the word *that*?   _____
5. Diagram the sentence on another sheet of paper.

11.8 **A nocturnal animal is one that is active at night.**
1. What is the simple subject?   _____
2. Which words are adjectives?   _____
3. What is the adjective clause?   _____
4. What word does this clause describe?   _____
5. Diagram the sentence on another sheet of paper.

11.9 **Laura is excited because everyone is coming to her violin recital.**
1. How is the word *excited* used in the sentence? _____
2. Is the adverb clause dependent or independent? _____
3. What is the adverb phrase? _____
4. What kind of pronoun is the word *everyone*? _____
5. Diagram the sentence on another sheet of paper.

11.10 **On rainy days we always hope that Mom will give us a ride to school.**
1. How is *On rainy days* used in the sentence? _____
2. How is the noun clause used in the sentence? _____
3. What part of speech is the word *always*? _____
4. What is the antecedent of the pronoun *us*? _____
5. Diagram the sentence on another sheet of paper.

11.11 **During the summer my brother Gary plans to work as a lifeguard on weekends.**
1. What is the appositive? _____
2. Is the appositive restrictive or nonrestrictive? _____
3. How is the infinitive used in the sentence? _____
4. Which words are prepositions? _____
5. Diagram the sentence on another sheet of paper.

11.1 Simple Sentences

A **diagram** is a visual outline of a sentence. It shows the relationships among words in a sentence. Diagramming shows how a sentence is put together. It identifies errors in a sentence and makes clear why they are errors.

Diagram the sentences.

1. A violet is a small purple flower.

2. My grandma sent me some new clothes.

3. We recently named the frisky brown colt Smarty.

4. A cat with a striped tail ran very quickly under the bushes.

For additional help, review pages 196–197 in your textbook or visit www.voyagesinenglish.com.

11.2 Appositives

An **appositive** is a word or a group of words that follows a noun or a pronoun and further identifies it or adds information. An appositive names the same person, place, thing, or idea as the word it explains.

Diagram the sentences.

1. The mythical hall of the dead, Valhalla, has many doors.

2. This is my brilliant math teacher, Mr. Gomez.

3. In the play the main character is transported to Oz, a fantastic land.

4. Ben enthusiastically read J.K. Rowling's novel *Harry Potter and the Goblet of Fire*.

For additional help, review pages 198–199 in your textbook or visit www.voyagesinenglish.com.

11.3 Compound Sentences

A **compound sentence** contains two or more independent clauses.
An independent clause has a subject and a predicate and can stand on its own as a sentence.

Diagram the sentences.

1. The tourists visited Washington, D.C., and they toured the Lincoln Memorial.

2. Megan ordered a new computer, but it was delivered to her previous address.

3. Emanuel's stories are creative; however, they are often based on real events.

4. Maria prefers autobiographies, yet she frequently reads adventure stories.

For additional help, review pages 200–201 in your textbook or visit www.voyagesinenglish.com.

Section 11 • 121

11.4 Compound Sentence Elements

The subject and the predicate in a sentence may be compound. They may consist of two or more words connected by a coordinating conjunction.

Diagram the sentences.

1. This old silk pillow is smooth and soft.

2. Molly and Grace make their own beds and fold their own laundry.

3. The club president called or visited each member of the committee.

4. Craig and Joe wrote the music and the lyrics for this song.

For additional help, review pages 202–203 in your textbook or visit www.voyagesinenglish.com.

11.5   Participles

> A **participle** is a verb form that is used as an adjective. A participial phrase is made up of the participle, its objects or complements, and any modifiers. The entire phrase acts as an adjective.

Diagram the sentences.

1. A smiling woman opened the locked door.

2. Tripping over the exposed tree root, I fell backwards.

3. The Renoir painting, displayed in a room with an expensive security system, is priceless.

4. Walking through the garden, we saw blooming flowers in a wide range of colors.

For additional help, review pages 204–205 in your textbook or visit www.voyagesinenglish.com.

Section 11 • 123

11.6 Gerunds

A **gerund** is a verb form ending in *ing* that is used as a noun. A gerund can be used in a sentence as a subject, a subject complement, an object of a verb, an object of a preposition, or an appositive.

Diagram the sentences.

1. Diagramming sentences is a useful writing tool.

2. Gabe and T.J. enjoyed playing the game.

3. Miles easily won the competition by creating the best robot.

4. My goal, earning money for college, will require hard work.

For additional help, review pages 206–207 in your textbook or visit www.voyagesinenglish.com.

© Loyola Press. Voyages in English   Grade 7

11.7 Infinitives

An **infinitive** is a verb form, usually preceded by *to*, that is used as a noun, an adjective, or an adverb.

Diagram the sentences.

1. Our soccer team wants to score many points in this game.

2. Most students were anxious to see the final test results.

3. My idea, to hold a raffle, will raise money for charity.

4. To survive this powerful storm was their primary concern.

© Loyola Press. Voyages in English   Grade 7

For additional help, review pages 208–209 in your textbook or visit www.voyagesinenglish.com.

11.8 Adjective Clauses

An **adjective clause** is a dependent clause that describes a noun or a pronoun. An adjective clause begins with a relative pronoun or with a subordinate conjunction.

Diagram the sentences.

1. Jim gave her the ring that he had brought from London.

2. This is the woman whose dog won the blue ribbon.

3. The artist who painted this lovely portrait lives in Mexico.

4. The department store where my brother currently works is having a sale.

For additional help, review pages 210–211 in your textbook or visit www.voyagesinenglish.com.

11.9 Adverb Clauses

An **adverb clause** is a dependent clause that acts as an adverb; it describes a verb, an adjective, or another adverb. Adverb clauses begin with subordinate conjunctions.

Diagram the sentences.

1. Mrs. Hamaguchi canceled the birthday party because her daughter was sick.

2. Since Toby received the highest test score, he has new confidence in his math skills.

3. If Greg studies for another hour, he will finally finish his homework.

4. Maya's sister will call you whenever she needs a ride to school.

For additional help, review pages 212–213 in your textbook or visit www.voyagesinenglish.com.

11.10 Noun Clauses

Dependent clauses can be used as nouns. **Noun clauses** work in sentences in the same way that nouns do.

Diagram the sentences.

1. Billy now recalls why he kept his notebook from the previous school year.

2. That the animal is dangerous and unpredictable seems obvious.

3. The fact that she was intelligent could not be denied.

4. Whoever uses the new sports equipment should be appreciative.

For additional help, review pages 214–215 in your textbook or visit www.voyagesinenglish.com.

11.11 Diagramming Practice

Diagramming shows the relationships among words in a sentence. It shows how a sentence is put together.

Read the diagrams and write out the sentences.

1. _____

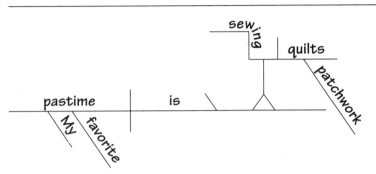

2. _____

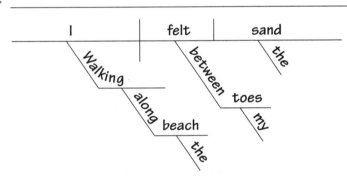

3. _____

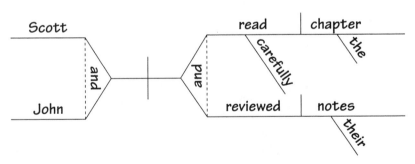

4. _____

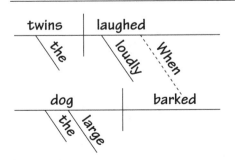

For additional help, review pages 216–217 in your textbook or visit www.voyagesinenglish.com.

What Makes a Good Personal Narrative?

> A **personal narrative** is a true story about a particular event written by the person who experienced it.

Read each statement. Circle *T* if the statement is true or *F* if the statement is false. Then rewrite each false statement to make it true.

1. A personal narrative tells about events that really happened.   T   F

   _____

2. A personal narrative is written in the third person.   T   F

   _____

3. The events of a personal narrative are written in a random order.   T   F

   _____

4. A personal narrative should flow smoothly from beginning to end.   T   F

   _____

5. A good topic would be one that the writer thinks is a bit interesting.   T   F

   _____

Write *yes* or *no* to show whether each idea would be an appropriate topic for a personal narrative.

6. instructions on how to build a bookshelf from wood   _____

7. the morning I discovered that someone had stolen my bike   _____

8. my day volunteering at the hospital   _____

9. a tourist's favorite places to visit in Washington, D.C.   _____

Write the tone of each passage.

10. "Stop!" I screamed, as I lunged to grab his jacket.   _____

11. "Look! Spring *must* be coming. The robin has returned!"   _____

12. Swimming in the warm river, my cares floated away.   _____

13. It was a clean snap! The quarterback made a break for it.   _____

14. Suddenly a wave of sorrow seemed to wash over me.   _____

15. I paused at that alley entrance, unable to see a thing.   _____

For additional help, review pages 224–227 in your textbook or visit www.voyagesinenglish.com.

© Loyola Press. Voyages in English   Grade 7

LESSON 2

Introduction, Body, and Conclusion

A good personal narrative has an **introduction,** a **body,** and a **conclusion.**

For each part of a personal narrative, write the letter of the matching description.

1. introduction _____   a. leaves the reader feeling satisfied and prompts the reader to think

2. body _____   b. tells what happened in chronological order

3. conclusion _____   c. sets the scene for the narrative

Read these mixed-up sentences from a personal narrative. Number the events in the logical order. Then circle the introduction and underline the conclusion.

4. After I put on my boots and skis, I took a lesson.   _____

5. I started down the mountain balancing on one leg.   _____

6. I will never forget the first time I went skiing.   _____

7. After a two-hour lesson, I felt confident to approach the chairlift.   _____

8. As I attempted to get out of the chairlift, my left ski came off.   _____

9. After that experience, I can safely say that two skis are better than one!   _____

10. Luckily, my instructor retrieved my left ski and handed it to me on her way down.   _____

11. The ride up on the chairlift made me feel calm as I gazed at the mountain scenery.   _____

12. I reached for my left ski, but unfortunately my right ski did not want to stop.   _____

13. The mountain scenery remained, but that calm feeling suddenly changed.   _____

Write a new introductory sentence for the above personal narrative. Then compare your introduction to the original, and tell how each is alike and different.

_____

_____

_____

Rewrite each sentence to make it a better concluding sentence.

14. I was pretty happy with the way the day turned out.

_____

15. I decided not to go back the next day.

_____

For additional help, review pages 228–231 in your textbook or visit www.voyagesinenglish.com.

Chapter 1 • 131

Revising Sentences

Revising sentences can help eliminate sentences that ramble or run on. **Rambling sentences** and **run-on sentences** make your writing harder to understand. You can avoid these kinds of sentences by being concise.

Each sentence pair has a rambling sentence and a run-on sentence. Circle the letter of the rambling sentence. Use proofreading marks to correct each sentence.

1. **a.** Larry walked onto the stage his heart began to pound very fast.

   b. He could not speak and he had a look of fear on his face, so Mrs. Burke began whispering his lines to him.

2. **a.** Fifteen students bought sweatshirts with the school logo, but the Pep Club still had dozens left to sell, and they had to be sold by the end of the day.

   b. Shaina had the idea that improved sales each fan received a magnet for every sweatshirt sold.

3. **a.** With the team down by one point and two seconds to go, Jenna was fouled as she went up for the shot, and the ball went in and out of the basket.

   b. The referee handed her the ball at the free-throw line she bounced it four times and then made her first free throw.

4. **a.** One of the first things the new teacher did was smile at each student she wanted each child to feel comfortable.

   b. Little Jamie waited until the bell rang and ran up and gave Miss Cross a picture that he had drawn in class, and Miss Cross taped the picture to her desk.

5. **a.** The women spent the day shopping at the mall and they spotted many bargains, but they did not buy anything.

   b. Ursula looked at the glossy, polished diamond ring in the window the sign noted that the ring was on sale.

Delete the redundant words in each sentence.

6. She was intent on eliminating and purging the redundant words in her writing.

7. Abby stared into the empty, vacant den and wondered where the wild wolves had gone.

8. Their host was courteous and interesting, while also being polite and sympathetic.

9. The costume was outlandish and bizarre, but Josh wasn't sure what was wrong with that.

10. "Ordinarily," I stammered, "Usually we start with a math warm-up and begin the lesson."

11. I was startled and frightened to see that my path was blocked by an enormous, tall man.

© Loyola Press. Voyages in English Grade 7

For additional help, review pages 232–235 in your textbook or visit www.voyagesinenglish.com.

LESSON
4

Exact Words

Exact words convey a specific, intended meaning to the reader. Precise words also help create more vivid visual images for the reader.

Circle the two words that are more specific examples of each word in bold type.

1. **house**	home	mansion	shack	residence
2. **animal**	camel	hyena	creature	beast
3. **vehicle**	motorcycle	ride	chariot	transportation
4. **flower**	plant	rose	daisy	blossom
5. **build**	make	form	assemble	construct
6. **strong**	potent	able	robust	big
7. **old**	dated	aged	decrepit	antique
8. **throw**	send	propel	fling	lift
9. **little**	diminutive	small	mini	microscopic
10. **chair**	seat	throne	furniture	recliner

Underline the homophone that correctly completes each sentence.

11. Kate couldn't believe how (callous, callus) the instructor was being.

12. When Raul went to the (sight, cite, site) on the Internet, it crashed his computer.

13. The old house had a laundry (chute, shoot) down which the boys tossed their dirty clothes.

14. I tried to (ring, wring) out the mop into the bucket, but the water went everywhere.

15. The construction workers decided to (raise, raze, rays) the dilapidated building.

Write the homophone that matches each definition. Use a dictionary if necessary.

16. to cover completely; not *rap* but . . . _____

17. to make an appearance; not *presents* but . . . _____

18. related to that military; not *marshal* but . . . _____

19. to sell something; not *pedal* but . . . _____

20. to look back; not *revue* but . . . _____

21. a juvenile; not *miner* but . . . _____

22. to be pulled tight; not *taught* but . . . _____

23. an officer in the Army or Air Force; not *kernel* but . . . _____

© Loyola Press. Voyages in English   Grade 7

For additional help, review pages 236–239 in your textbook or visit www.voyagesinenglish.com.

Chapter 1 • 133

Graphic Organizers

A **graphic organizer** can help writers map out their ideas. A graphic
organizer can help arrange subtopics and details related to a chosen topic.
It also keeps writers from introducing unnecessary details.

**Complete the time line. Add only the dates and events you consider most important
to your life.**

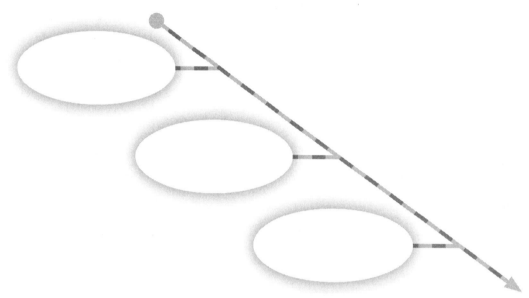

**Fill in the word web below using an experience from your own life. Add more ovals
if you need to.**

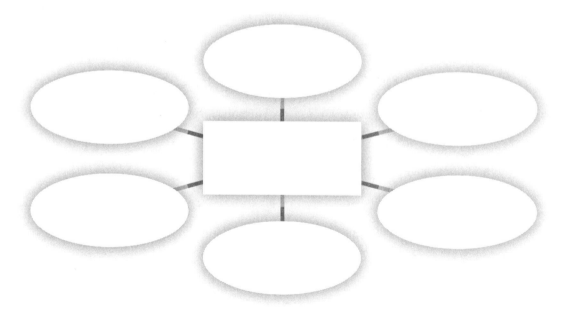

For additional help, review pages 240–243 in your textbook
or visit www.voyagesinenglish.com.

What Makes a Good Business Letter?

A **business letter** is a formal letter with a business-related purpose. It includes a heading, an inside address, a salutation, the body, and a closing.

Circle the words that correctly complete the sentences in this paragraph.

A letter of application is a type of (**1.** personal   business) letter. It is
(**2.** a formal   an informal) letter that has a (**3.** general   specific)
purpose. The purpose of a letter of application is to apply for
a (**4.** job   license). This kind of letter should always be
(**5.** long and rambling   short and to the point).

Evaluate the sentences for appropriateness in a business letter. Cross out extraneous information. Then on another sheet of paper, rewrite the sentences that require a more professional tone.

6. I am sooo glad I picked your company from which to buy this little widget!

7. I am writing to express my displeasure with the service I received at store #103 on Tuesday, May 3. Of course, I write a lot of letters, but maybe you will actually answer this one.

8. Hi, I hope this letter finds you well. I am writing to thank you for your company's generous donation to our school fund-raiser. The family fun passes were very popular with bidders.

9. I received my order in the mail today. What were you thinking? This isn't a water dish; it's a swimming pool! I am returning the "dish." Please send me my refund.

10. We admire your company's dedication to the community and want to know how we can help. I really love to sing. Is there any way I can do something like that to help?

11. I am writing to explain my part in the events of last weekend. It is totally unfair that I am being blamed for the damage that was done. It's true I was there, but I was one of the people telling others that they should go find something else to do.

12. I want to work for your company. Could I come in and meet with someone to talk about that? Anytime would be cool with me.

13. Hey. We just want to say a big "Thank You!" for all the stuff you gave our club for the spring play. You guys totally rock!

14. Please accept this letter of recommendation for Raul Porras. He is one of my best friends. Raul is responsible. He can be counted on to stay positive under pressure. He is also a professional and friendly employee. In fact, we count on him to welcome newcomers.

15. I am writing to request a copy of my last bill. I seem to have lost mine. I'm sorry about that.

For additional help, review pages 262–265 in your textbook
or visit www.voyagesinenglish.com.

Chapter 2 • 135

LESSON
2

Purpose, Audience, and Tone

A business letter should be written with the **purpose, audience,** and **tone** in mind. State your purpose early in the body and choose words appropriate for your audience and the tone you want to convey.

Write *application, request, gratitude,* or *complaint* to identify the purpose of each statement.

1. We would be grateful if you would consider visiting this fall. _____

2. Unfortunately, the product does not meet our expectations. _____

3. The gift you sent brought tears of joy to Mom's eyes. _____

4. My experience is uniquely suited to the demands of the job. _____

5. I believe my dedication to assisting elderly people makes me an excellent match for this position. _____

6. We found your simple gesture to be profoundly thoughtful. _____

7. Please think about donating a family pack of movie passes. _____

8. This kind of customer service is simply not acceptable. _____

Write an appropriate tone for each topic.

9.
> **Purpose:** You are applying to be a lifeguard at a pool. You summarize your swimming ability and safety training.
> **Audience:** Bill Mueller, the head lifeguard at the pool
> **Tone:** _____

10.
> **Purpose:** You are complaining to the manufacturer about a leaky hummingbird feeder. You describe when and where you bought the feeder and your experience in trying to use it.
> **Audience:** a customer service representative
> **Tone:** _____

11.
> **Purpose:** You are asking your uncle to send you a copy of the science-fiction novel he wrote. You describe science-fiction novels you've read and liked before.
> **Audience:** your favorite uncle
> **Tone:** _____

© Loyola Press. Voyages in English   **Grade 7**

For additional help, review pages 266–269 in your textbook or visit www.voyagesinenglish.com.

LESSON
3

Adjective Clauses

Adjective clauses modify a noun or a pronoun and usually begin with a relative pronoun. Adjective clauses can improve your writing by shifting the emphasis, deepening the meaning, or increasing the variety of sentences.

Underline each adjective clause.

1. My brother, who is three years older than I, turned 13 last weekend.

2. My parents, who are normally strict, allowed him to get a pet of his own.

3. My brother was speechless, which is pretty unusual.

4. Carl, whom my brother called to tell about the gift, came running over to our house.

5. Dad turned onto the road that goes the past the school to get to the shelter.

6. The car wouldn't start, which is fairly typical.

7. We got in the van, which is in much better condition, and set off for the shelter.

8. It was lunchtime at the shelter, which is why all the dogs were barking, when we arrived.

9. We talked to the director who is in charge of adoptions and offered our help.

10. Pretty soon all the animals were quiet, which was a relief.

11. My brother, who had fallen silent, was staring at a group of cats.

12. The cats that were all in the first cage were mostly eating.

13. One cat that was gray and white was staring back at us.

14. It reached out a paw, which was the funniest gesture, as though it was waving at us.

15. My brother named the cat Tiger, which is a great name for a cat, and we brought it home.

Complete each sentence with an adjective clause that shifts the emphasis, deepens the meaning, or adds variety.

16. Breakfast, _____, was a big meal.

17. His father, _____, was one of nine children.

18. I did not know you have a horse _____.

19. The team's mascot, _____, is called Clinky.

20. The man _____ is the one to ask.

On another sheet of paper, write three descriptive sentences. Use an adjective clause in each sentence.

For additional help, review pages 270–273 in your textbook or visit www.voyagesinenglish.com.

Chapter 2 • 137

LESSON 4

Roots

A **root** is the base from which a word is built. Looking for a root inside a word can help you understand its meaning.

Underline the root in each italicized word. Write the letter of the matching root meaning. Use a dictionary if you need help. Then think about what your response would be to each sentence.

1. Name two things you *transport* to school. _____ a. life

2. Name two things a jeweler might *inscribe* on a ring. _____ b. listen

3. Name two *aquatic* animals. _____ c. people

4. Name two things you study in *biology*. _____ d. carry

5. Name two sounds you might hear in an *auditorium*. _____ e. write

6. Name two events you have attended as a *spectator*. _____ f. watch

7. Name two *epidemics* that have happened in the past. _____ g. water

8. Name two things you might see at a *graduation*. _____ h. step

Use each root to help you find the appropriate word to complete each sentence.

flect: meaning "bend."

9. Amber noticed how the light _____ off the clean glass.

10. Somehow Audrey managed to _____ all the criticism and stay positive.

gram: meaning "letter" or "written."

11. The teacher's focus on _____ helped the class improve its writing over the year.

12. Eduardo decided to draw a _____ to better communicate the idea in his report.

migr: meaning "change" or "move."

13. Every winter the birds _____ to a warmer climate.

14. Many _____ to America work hard and hope to become productive citizens.

Study each word's root. Then write the meaning for each word on another sheet of paper. Use a dictionary as needed.

15. remiss
16. symphony
17. infinite
18. podium
19. photogenic
20. advocate
21. sanitation
22. query
23. appendix

© Loyola Press. Voyages in English Grade 7

For additional help, review pages 274–277 in your textbook or visit www.voyagesinenglish.com.

LESSON
5

Writing Tools

A **summary** is a condensed version of a text or other source, written in your own words. **Paraphrasing** is restating individual passages in a more detailed way than a summary. A **direct quotation** contains words identical to the original text.

Read each passage. Then identify the italicized text as a summary or a paraphrased piece and explain your answer.

1. **Passage:** Superman was the original comic-book superhero. At his inception in 1938, he was faster than a speeding bullet, more powerful than a locomotive, and could leap tall buildings in a single bound. However, he could not fly until 1941.

   Superman was introduced in 1938 with all the powers he has today, except he could not fly.

   _____

   _____

2. **Passage:** *The War of the Worlds* was a radio play based on a short story written by H.G. Wells. Many listeners who tuned into the show late missed the explanation that the radio show was fictional. They believed that the announcer and reporter in the show were real and that the events being reported, that Martians were invading Earth, were really happening.

   The War of the Worlds is a short story by H.G. Wells about Martians invading Earth. It was turned into a radio play. Even though it was announced that the show was fictional, some listeners missed this part. They believed that the events were actually occurring.

   _____

   _____

3. **Passage:** In 1945 Pennsylvania engineer Richard James was at home working with springs on a military invention. When he accidentally knocked one of the long, coiled springs off a bookshelf, he got the idea of marketing it as a toy instead. The inventor's wife, Betty, named the toy "Slinky." The Slinky has changed little since it was first introduced.

   A Pennsylvania engineer accidentally invented the Slinky in 1945 when he knocked a long, coiled spring off a bookshelf.

   _____

   _____

4. What are some similarities and differences between a summary and paraphrasing?

   _____

   _____

For additional help, review pages 278–281 in your textbook or visit www.voyagesinenglish.com.

Chapter 2 • 139

What Makes a Good How-to Article?

How-to writing is a kind of expository writing. How-to writing provides information that explains how to do or make something.

Read the article. Then answer the questions.

Feeling bored on a windy day? Then go fly a kite. The first thing you need to do is get a kite and a large ball of string. Read the directions that came with your kite to find out how to put it together and how to attach the string. Next, take your kite to a large, open area with no tree branches or overhead power lines. Determine which way the wind is blowing. Then hold your kite as high as you can so the wind can lift it. As the wind catches the kite, begin to let out your string. Then start walking backward to keep the string tight. If your kite is stable, let out more string to make it fly higher. When you are ready to go home, slowly wind up the string and bring down your kite.

1. What is the purpose of this how-to paragraph?

   _____

2. Why are the sentences written as steps?

   _____

   _____

3. What is the first step when you fly a kite?

   _____

4. What should you do after you find a large, open space?

   _____

5. Provide an example from the paragraph of a sentence in the imperative mood.

   _____

6. What materials or tools has the author specified?

   _____

7. This article might be found in a book about kites. Where else might you find how-to articles?

   _____

   _____

For additional help, review pages 300–303 in your textbook or visit www.voyagesinenglish.com.

© Loyola Press. Voyages in English   Grade 7

LESSON 2

Relevant Details

> **Relevant details** support the topic of a how-to article. A paragraph has unity when every detail relates to the topic sentence or main idea.

Choose a how-to topic from this list. Write the steps needed to complete the activity. If you have more than six steps, list them on another sheet of paper. Then answer the questions.

How to multiply two-digit numbers   How to upload a document

How to make your favorite snack   How to fix a flat tire

1.   STEP 1

STEP 2

STEP 3

STEP 4

STEP 5

STEP 6

2. My most explicit details are _____ .

3. The intended audience is _____ .

4. The relevant details are arranged in _____ order.

5. My article would be clearer if I _____ .

On another sheet of paper, use your steps to write a how-to paragraph. Exchange papers with a partner and look for any misfit sentences.

For additional help, review pages 304–307 in your textbook or visit www.voyagesinenglish.com.

Chapter 3 • 141

LESSON
3

Transition Words

> **Transition words** connect ideas in a logical order. These words help the details in a how-to article flow smoothly.

Use the transition words in the box to complete the sentences. Use a variety of words, but repeat some words if they make the most sense.

above	after	because	before	behind	but	consequently	finally
first	however	instead	later	next	now	therefore	soon
still	then	so	yet	last	under	in conclusion	again

1. Cream the mixture _____ adding butter, eggs, and sugar to the bowl.

2. Use cotton if available; _____, this pattern will work for silk as well.

3. _____, I hope I have convinced you that anyone can cook a great quiche.

4. Tussah silk has a different texture _____ the silkworms eat real leaves.

5. Knead the dough _____, this time for only five minutes.

6. _____, you can add a coat of clear varnish for durability.

7. _____, allow the bread to cool for 10 minutes before removing it from the pan.

8. _____ starting the engine, carefully adjust the choke.

9. Don't add the vanilla _____; wait until after the fudge is boiling rapidly.

10. _____, lay out your materials on the table so each is easy to grab.

11. Place the second paper cutout _____ the first one and glue together.

12. Pick up the second wrench _____, and use it to secure the bolts.

13. _____ congratulate yourself on assembling your very own laser pointer.

Choose one of the topics below. On another sheet of paper, write a how-to paragraph about your topic. Use at least five transition words in your paragraph.

A. You have developed a surefire strategy for earning high scores on a popular computer game. Write a paragraph that explains the first three steps in your strategy.

B. You want to make your favorite meal for dinner. Describe the first three steps you take to prepare the meal.

C. You are a guest instructor at a sports camp. It is your job to demonstrate how to perform a sports skill and teach a group of eight-year-olds how to perform it. Write a paragraph that explains the first three things you will do.

© Loyola Press. Voyages in English Grade 7

For additional help, review pages 308–311 in your textbook or visit www.voyagesinenglish.com.

LESSON
4

Adverb Clauses

An **adverb clause** usually modifies a verb, though it can also modify an adjective or another adverb. Adverb clauses are used to add variety or change the meaning of a sentence and are introduced by subordinate conjunctions.

Underline the adverb clauses. Circle the word or words each clause modifies.

1. The alarm went off because the exit door was opened.
2. If you make Jan a card, maybe she will help you with your homework.
3. Kyle has been arriving at school on time since he started jogging in the morning.
4. The puppy barked until the bearded man held out his hand.
5. After the mulberry bush was damaged, the gardener planted a new bush.
6. Put on your shoes before you stub your toe on the sidewalk.
7. So that everyone gets a turn, each person will speak for only five minutes.
8. We all can go on the field trip, provided everyone turns in a permission slip.

Revise each sentence pair by making one sentence an adverb clause.

9. My aunt introduced me to pickled okra. I don't know how I had lived without it.

   _____

10. Check the pan carefully for cracks. Pour the batter into the pan.

    _____

11. Don't try to start the engine. Reconnect the throttle cable.

    _____

12. You are attending the drama club meeting. You can bring the box of costumes.

    _____

13. They will harden as they cool. The cookies may appear raw in the middle.

    _____

Complete each sentence with an appropriate adverb clause.

14. While _____ , the kitchen smelled like apples.

15. Her suitcase looked _____ .

16. When _____ , the dancers began their routine.

17. Call your parents if _____ .

18. From the brush the lion watched the zebras until _____ .

For additional help, review pages 312–315 in your textbook or visit www.voyagesinenglish.com.

© Loyola Press. Voyages in English   Grade 7

Chapter 3 • 143

Dictionary

A **dictionary** contains an alphabetical list of words. For each word, the entry includes the definition, the syllabication, the part of speech, and the pronunciation.

Look up each italicized word in a dictionary. On another sheet of paper, write the definition that best fits the context of the sentence.

1. Michael *bristled* at the insinuation that he had cheated on the exam.
2. Suspecting a *bug*, the spy carefully dismantled the lamp to find the tiny wires.
3. We sorted the bills by their *denominations*.
4. They did everything to keep the flowers alive, but in the end the drought *prevailed*.
5. Our class staged a mock *summit* at the same time the world leaders were meeting.
6. The *tone* of the colors in the painting gave it a melancholy mood.
7. The president put Governor Rasband in charge of *affairs* of the state.
8. We were all encouraged to avoid *cheap* jokes in the talent show.
9. The family was a bit alarmed when Grandma decided to paint her bathroom a *deep* purple.
10. Don't *interfere* with the children's attempts to solve the problem on their own.

Find the meaning of each word. Write a sentence that illustrates its meaning.

11. feign

_____

12. fiasco

_____

Use the sample dictionary entry below to answer the questions that follow.

de • mean (di-**mēn**) *tr. v.* 1. To conduct or behave in a particular manner. [From Old French *demener*] 2. To lower, as in dignity or social standing: *The dog refused to demean herself by eating out of the trash.* [From English *mean*, to humble] **de • meaned, de • mean • ing, de • means**

13. What part of speech is *demean*? _____
14. How many syllables does *demean* have? _____
15. How many meanings does *demean* have? _____

On another sheet of paper, write two sentences using *demean*. Each sentence should demonstrate a different meaning.

For additional help, review pages 316–319 in your textbook or visit www.voyagesinenglish.com.

© Loyola Press. Voyages in English Grade 7

LESSON
1

What Makes a Good Description?

Descriptive writing uses vivid vocabulary to portray a person, a place, or a thing. A good **description** will capture a reader's senses and imagination.

Complete each sentence with information about descriptive writing.

1. Descriptive writing gives the reader _____.

2. A good thing to do before writing a description is to picture _____ and consider _____.

3. Writing a description is like painting _____ for the reader.

4. In descriptive writing, the author sets a mood or creates _____.

5. _____ is a more vivid, exact word for *clean*.

6. _____ is a more vivid, exact word for *nice*.

7. _____ is an example of a word that appeals to the sense of touch.

8. _____ is an example of a word that appeals to the sense of sound.

Read each topic, picture the scene in your mind, and write three descriptive words you could use to describe the scene you visualized.

9. rainy night

_____   _____   _____

10. snowstorm

_____   _____   _____

11. walk on a windy day

_____   _____   _____

12. summer afternoon

_____   _____   _____

13. late autumn day

_____   _____   _____

Find an example of a descriptive paragraph. On another sheet of paper, answer the following questions about the paragraph.

14. What is the topic of the paragraph?

15. How did the writer help you visualize what was being described?

16. What was the mood of the description? List three words or phrases the writer used to convey the mood.

17. List two examples of words the writer used to appeal to the senses.

© Loyola Press. Voyages in English   Grade 7

For additional help, review pages 338–341 in your textbook or visit www.voyagesinenglish.com.

LESSON 2

Organization

Organize details so that one detail flows logically into the next. Depending on your topic, you may want to use different kinds of organization such as **spatial order, chronological order,** and **comparing and contrasting.**

Write whether you would organize each topic by *spatial order*, by *chronological order*, or by *comparing and contrasting*.

1. how my new game is better than my old one   _____

2. the interior of the International Space Station   _____

3. a visit to Ralph Waldo Emerson's home   _____

4. a trip to Japan and China   _____

5. the characters Voldemort and Uncle Olaf   _____

6. a birthday celebration   _____

7. a family vacation   _____

8. a sales brochure for a recreational vehicle   _____

Write details on this Venn diagram comparing and contrasting life in the city to life in the country.

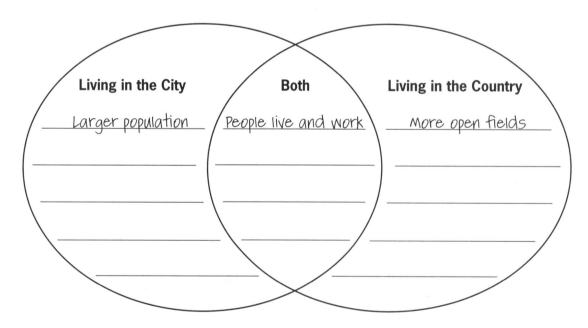

Living in the City
Larger population

Both
People live and work

Living in the Country
More open fields

On another sheet of paper, write five descriptive sentences comparing and contrasting life in the city to life in the country, using the ideas above.

For additional help, review pages 342–345 in your textbook or visit www.voyagesinenglish.com.

© Loyola Press. Voyages in English   Grade 7

LESSON
3

Noun Clauses

A **noun clause** is a dependent clause used as a noun. A noun clause can be used as a subject, a subject complement, a direct object, an object of a preposition, and an appositive.

Underline the noun clause in each sentence. Write whether the noun clause is used as a *subject*, a *subject complement*, a *direct object*, an *object of a preposition*, or an *appositive*.

1. We do not know where the lost puppy lives. _____

2. Please tell her how to get to the library. _____

3. The best time is whenever you want it to be. _____

4. Read the directions for what you should do next. _____

5. What the baby needs is a warm blanket. _____

6. Whoever swims the fastest will win the race. _____

7. The idea that we can complete this in one night is ludicrous. _____

8. A coat of paint will restore the room to how it used to look. _____

9. I love how my dog makes me feel when I get home. _____

10. The Baghetti brothers are who you should call for help. _____

11. Whichever soap you choose will do the job as well. _____

12. She will drive the horses that are white when she comes. _____

Use each set of words to write a sentence with a noun clause.

13. scientists believe, meteor may have caused climate changes

_____

14. everyone wondered, come through the door next

_____

15. bank will give a reward, supplies them with information about the robbery

_____

16. children are well prepared, seems obvious

_____

17. a sign of fitness, heart rate responds to brisk activity

_____

For additional help, review pages 346–349 in your textbook or visit www.voyagesinenglish.com.

Chapter 4 • 147

LESSON 4

Adjective and Adverb Suffixes

A **suffix** can change the function, or use, of a word. Suffixes added to nouns or verbs can create adjectives, nouns, or adverbs. A suffix that creates an adjective is an **adjective suffix**. An **adverb suffix** creates an adverb.

Write a suffix to complete each sentence. Use a dictionary if needed.

1. We gasped, feeling the plan was exceptionally audiac_____.

2. The cat's matern_____ instincts were obvious when she moved to protect the kitten.

3. We thought Norford was being a little self_____ not to share his art supplies.

4. Helen is the most act_____ of the six children.

5. Albert thoughtful_____ replaced the cap on the milk jug.

6. The scen_____ view from the cabin window enticed us to go outside.

7. The silk_____ texture of the fabric gave the dress an elegant appearance.

8. My brother virtuous_____ did not to eat any of the leftover dessert.

9. We found the new computer program to be trouble_____ and hard to use.

10. The barber careful_____ cleaned and stored the razors and scissors.

Write a new word made by adding an adjective suffix to each base word.

11. tact _____

12. vigil _____

13. assist _____

14. hero _____

15. negate _____

16. bother _____

17. nature _____

18. perish _____

19. grace _____

20. clear _____

21. differ _____

22. peril _____

Write a sentence using each base word and the suffix in parentheses.

23. pleasant (-ly)

_____

24. rebel (-ous)

_____

25. elude (-ive)

_____

For additional help, review pages 350–353 in your textbook or visit www.voyagesinenglish.com.

LESSON 5

Thesaurus

A **thesaurus** is a reference tool that gives synonyms for words.

Use a thesaurus to find synonyms for each word. Use the part of speech in parentheses to choose a synonym to complete each sentence.

flood

1. (verb) The water from the rain will _____ the lawns.

2. (noun) The _____ of water rushed over the bridge.

work

3. (noun) Moving the bed took a lot of _____.

4. (verb) Kenji will _____ the buttons on the control panel.

aid

5. (noun) The counselor's words will give the man the _____ he needs.

6. (verb) The vet will _____ the wounded animal if she can.

space

7. (verb) _____ the text evenly on your poster.

8. (noun) Give Enrique some _____ so he can catch his breath.

fair

9. (adjective) At the end of the story, the prince rescues the _____ maiden.

10. (noun) We can ride the Ferris wheel at the _____.

Underline the word in parentheses that best replaces the underlined word in each sentence.

11. John <u>said</u>, "Run! The kitchen is on fire!" (whispered   bellowed   sang   enunciated)

12. I thought the book was very <u>interesting</u>. (curious   absorbing   boring   appalling)

13. Honestly, I thought that the boy was <u>quite</u> rude. (unusually   routinely   completely   much)

14. Today's hot lunch was <u>good</u>. (edible   adequate   delectable   palatable)

15. Can you believe how <u>big</u> that cat is? (immense   mature   prominent   insignificant)

16. Last night's show was simply <u>amazing</u>. (regular   prodigious   ominous   mediocre)

17. Emily responded in a <u>haughty</u> tone of voice. (arrogant   tranquil   raucous   dainty)

© Loyola Press. Voyages in English Grade 7

For additional help, review pages 354–357 in your textbook or visit www.voyagesinenglish.com.

LESSON
1

What Makes a Good Book Review?

A **book review** gives information about a book and tells what the reviewer liked and disliked about it. A book review is more than a summary of a book; it is also an evaluation.

Read the book review. Then answer the questions.

At first when I read *The Giver*, I could not imagine a world like the one the main character, Jonas, lived in. Then I felt concern for Jonas as he had to make some extremely difficult choices.

In this utopian world, few people are given choices. Although he is young, Jonas is one of the people who is given the opportunity to explore creativity, to experience pain and love, and to make choices. Jonas wants to share what he experiences with everyone else.

The book is well written. Lois Lowry carefully creates an atmosphere in which the reader senses something is not quite right about this perfect world. Once it is clear exactly what is wrong, she keeps the reader in suspense. Lowry explores the theme of how feelings and emotions influence the choices we make. The ending is not perfectly clear because the reader chooses how to interpret it.

1. Underline the introduction. Why is this introduction effective, and how could it be improved?

   _____

   _____

2. Circle the section that summarizes the plot of the book.

3. How does the reviewer support his or her assertion that the book is well written?

   _____

4. What is the title, author, and genre of the book in the review?

   _____

5. What do you learn about the characters, setting, and theme?

   _____

   _____

6. What information do you think is missing from the review?

   _____

   _____

© Loyola Press. Voyages in English Grade 7

For additional help, review pages 376–379 in your textbook or visit www.voyagesinenglish.com.

LESSON 2

Writing a Book Review

A good book review includes important information about the characters, setting, and plot; identifies the theme; and gives an evaluation of the book.

Write a word to complete each statement about book reviews.

1. A book review often begins by describing the _____ and the setting.

2. Most of the body of a book review will _____ the plot of the book.

3. A _____ is the overall idea that a book develops.

4. The _____ gives the reviewer's opinions about the book and reasons to support those opinions.

Write what you learn about the main character and setting in each review.

> *Martin the Warrior,* by Brian Jacques, is a classic tale of good versus evil. Bedrang the stoat, an ermine, is the bad guy whose captive mouse is the courageous Martin the Warrior. Martin is the most famous mouse in all of Redwall, an ancient stone abbey.

5. Main character: _____

_____

6. Setting: _____

> *Holes,* by Louis Sachar, is an unusual story about unusual characters. The author describes a strange detention center where the teen inmates must dig holes for hours each day. In particular the tale follows the life of Stanley Yelnats and the story of his family, tracing the ancestors' lives as each endured the Yelnats curse.

7. Main character: _____

_____

8. Setting: _____

Circle the conclusion in the evaluation. Underline the reasons or examples that support the reviewer's conclusions.

9. Bill Bryson is an author of *A Really Short History of Nearly Everything,* a book for all ages. This is a science book that is written like a great story. In the first sentence of the book, he writes, "No matter how hard you try you will never be able to grasp just how tiny, how spatially unassuming, is a proton." That sentence makes me smile, but it also makes me want to learn more about protons—something I had never even heard of up until that point.

© Loyola Press. Voyages in English   Grade 7

For additional help, review pages 380–383 in your textbook or visit www.voyagesinenglish.com.

Chapter 5 • 151

Expanding and Combining Sentences

Good writers use a variety of sentences to keep the reader focused and interested. By **expanding and combining sentences,** writers vary sentence length and complexity and include more descriptive details.

Write additional details to expand these sentences to make them more interesting. Use the information in parentheses to help you add words.

1. Waves crashed. (adjective, adverb)

   _____

2. Kyra jumped. (adjective, prepositional phrase)

   _____

3. The dog barked. (adjective, adverb, prepositional phrase)

   _____

4. The students gasped. (adjective, adverb, noun)

   _____

5. The bird flew. (adjective, adverb, prepositional phrase)

   _____

Add words to complete the sentences in each pair. Then use a conjunction to combine the two sentences into a compound sentence.

6. Tourists visit _____. Tourists also visit _____.

   _____

7. Many inhabitants are _____. Others are _____.

   _____

8. Sudden storms come. The weather in _____ is mostly _____.

   _____

9. Most teenagers eat _____. They drink _____.

   _____

10. Take a drive in _____. You will see _____.

    _____

© Loyola Press. Voyages in English   Grade 7

For additional help, review pages 384–387 in your textbook or visit www.voyagesinenglish.com.

LESSON 4

Outlines

An **outline** is a plan for a piece of writing that helps you organize your ideas. An outline helps you focus each paragraph on one idea and makes sure that every detail in the paragraph supports that idea.

Complete each sentence by circling all the choices that are correct.

1. An outline is
   a. a plan for writing that helps you organize ideas.
   b. a tool to ensure each paragraph focuses on one idea and the details support that idea.
   c. a division of ideas that follows a specific format.
   d. an organizer that helps you compare and contrast your opinions.

2. To create an outline,
   a. begin by deciding on a main idea.
   b. use only complete sentences with correct punctuation and capitalization.
   c. label each main idea with a Roman numeral followed by a period.
   d. list subtopics under each main idea and the details under each subtopic.

3. Once an outline is created,
   a. it should not be rewritten or modified.
   b. it can help you see what ideas need further revision.
   c. check for balance to make sure items show equal importance.
   d. look for details that are out of place or do not belong.

Read the section of an outline and answer the questions.

> II. Body
>   A. Percy learns the truth.
>   1. Percy learns his father is the god Poseidon.
>   2. His best friend turns out to be a satyr who was sent to protect him.
>   3. He may be kicked out of school for fighting a monster.

4. What would you expect to come before this part of the outline? _____

5. What is the subtopic? _____

6. What are the supporting details? _____

_____

For additional help, review pages 388–391 in your textbook or visit www.voyagesinenglish.com.

Chapter 5 • 153

Prefixes

A **prefix** is a syllable or syllables added to the beginning of a word. A prefix changes the meaning of the word to which it is added.

Underline the prefix in each word and write its meaning.

1. extraordinary _____
2. immature _____
3. transcribe _____
4. misanthrope _____
5. superimpose _____
6. preamble _____
7. incorrect _____
8. postscript _____
9. antifreeze _____

Write the word from the box to match each definition.

preclude	postdate	superhuman	incomplete	misspell
transpolar	antibody	interact	misfortune	indirect

10. not finished _____
11. something that acts against a virus _____
12. rule out in advance _____
13. write or say wrong letters _____
14. talk or act among one another _____
15. more than average person _____
16. bad luck _____
17. not going straight to the point _____
18. across the North or South Pole _____
19. to date something later than the real date _____

Add an appropriate prefix, using those found in the exercises above, to each word below. Then write a sentence using each new word.

20. cede _____
21. accurate _____
22. caution _____
23. merge _____
24. calculate _____

© Loyola Press. Voyages in English   Grade 7

For additional help, review pages 392–395 in your textbook or visit www.voyagesinenglish.com.

What Makes Good Fantasy Fiction?

Fantasy fiction takes readers to places they have never experienced. It has a beginning, a middle, and an end that provide an organized pattern of events and a clear line between good and evil.

Read each statement. Circle *T* if the statement is true or *F* if it is false.

1.	Fantasy fiction is usually factual.	T	F
2.	The setting of a fantasy story may be a different world.	T	F
3.	The plot of a fantasy story is usually told out of sequence.	T	F
4.	The problem or conflict is introduced toward the end.	T	F
5.	The plot is usually developed in the middle of the fantasy story.	T	F
6.	The series of spiraling events in fantasy fiction is called the climax.	T	F
7.	The main character achieves his or her goal at the end of a fantasy story.	T	F

Write *C* if each passage introduces a character and *S* if it introduces the setting. Some passages may do both.

8. Hadley looked out at the rain-soaked scene from under the relative dryness of her home's doorway. The heavy mist that accompanied the rain this time of year meant she couldn't see far out over the sea, but she thought maybe those black dots might be something. Yes, she was sure they were moving. Her heart began to beat faster. Were those ships? _____

9. Chiara got unsteadily to her feet. What had happened? Where was everyone? She felt about to cry but took a deep breathe and then held it for a few seconds. Pull yourself together, she told herself. She was in a kind of underground cave. Light filtered in from above. Did I fall from up there? she wondered. The thought lifted her spirits a bit. She congratulated herself on being tough enough to survive that kind of fall. Then she began to look around for handholds. She knew she needed to get out of the cave. _____

10. Cascading down the rocky slope were thousands of waterfalls, weaving in and out of each other like an ever-changing dance of light. The setting sun gave the water a shimmering glow so that the young elf wondered for a moment if there might be gold under the surface. _____

11. Claude felt uneasy when he saw the castle walls. He was to go in through the main entrance and ask for Lord Phillipe, but he was overwhelmed by the feeling that this was a trap. Instinctively, he put his hand over the pocket sewn into his coat. The message wasn't for Lord Phillipe, but for his daughter. Claude jumped off his horse and rolled in the dusty road. He unbraided the horse's tail and removed the brass decorations from the saddle and bridle, working methodically until there were no signs left of his life as a prince. _____

For additional help, review pages 414–417 in your textbook or visit www.voyagesinenglish.com.

Chapter 6 • 155

Plot Development

A good fantasy story includes a problem for the main character to face, obstacles to overcome, the dramatic moment toward which the story builds, and a satisfying resolution.

Write a word to complete each statement about the plot of a fantasy.

1. The _____ comes after the problem is solved and ties up any loose ends.

2. After the hero rid the town of bothersome dragons, he discovered the real enemy was an evil wizard. This is a summary of the story's _____.

3. The _____ is the most dramatic moment of the story when the main character finally solves or faces his or her problem.

4. The main character may face many problems, but one is a fundamental issue that thwarts the hero from accomplishing his or her goals. This is called the story's _____.

Identify the conflict and resolution in each summary of a fantasy story.

Nima lives on a desert planet where widely scattered oases are the only support for a group of colonies. A new virus sweeps through her colony, so Nima and her friends set out to find help. One friend falls ill, but Nima finds the cure. Unfortunately, a sandstorm destroys the vehicle in which they were traveling, so Nima uses her wits to return in time to save lives.

5. Conflict: _____

6. Resolution: _____

Umi and Oni are royalty in an ancient African kingdom when they stumble across a way to travel forward in time. Umi searches desperately for a way to get home again, but Oni quickly adapts to modern life and doesn't want to return. Umi learns to make peace with the fact that this is her brother's decision, and Oni comes to see how his sister can take what she learned in the present and use it to improve the past. When they do find the way home, they return united and wiser.

7. Conflict: _____

8. Resolution: _____

For additional help, review pages 418–421 in your textbook or visit www.voyagesinenglish.com.

LESSON
3

Dialogue

Dialogue adds interest to a scene by helping readers feel that they are right in the middle of the action. Dialogue is also an effective way of conveying emotion, humor, and subtle information about the characters.

Write nine words that can replace the word *said* and help describe the manner in which a character speaks.

1. _____   4. _____   7. _____

2. _____   5. _____   8. _____

3. _____   6. _____   9. _____

Read the dialogue and answer the questions.

"Miguel and Tam, sitting in a tree," sang Elena in a singsong voice.
"Stop!" Miguel yelled, and then more softly he continued, "That's not funny, Elena. Tam is my friend and she's very sick."
Elena looked surprised. "It's not—, I didn't mean—," she stammered, growing red-faced. Finally, she sighed, "I'm sorry, Miguel."

10. Which character is probably younger? Why? _____

_____

11. How does the author use dialogue to show that the characters know each other well?

_____

_____

Add punctuation to the dialogue for the first character. Then write a response of dialogue for the second character.

12. Description: two children flying on an airplane for the first time

Look at how small the houses seem squealed Bridget

_____

13. Description: a paramedic helping a man in a car accident

Do you think my leg is broken Jonathan cried

_____

14. Description: a comic-book hero confronting a villain

So hissed the evildoer you think you can foil my diabolical plan do you

_____

For additional help, review pages 422–425 in your textbook or visit www.voyagesinenglish.com.

Chapter 6 • 157

Figurative Language

Figurative language compares one thing to another in a way that adds interest and insight to the comparison.

Complete each sentence with the figure of speech in parentheses.

1. The tumbleweeds _____. (personification)

2. This pile of dirty clothes is _____. (hyperbole)

3. The baby's skin is _____. (simile)

4. Our new house is _____. (metaphor)

5. The flowers _____ in the breeze. (personification)

6. During the summer, the gym is _____. (simile)

7. That final exam was _____. (metaphor)

8. The chair _____ under the man's weight. (personification)

9. It's so cold today that _____. (hyperbole)

10. After the triathlon, my body _____. (simile)

11. My brother's old clunker of a car was _____. (metaphor)

Rewrite each sentence by replacing the underlined cliché with more effective figurative language.

12. We tried to eat the bread rolls, but they were <u>hard as rocks</u>.

_____

13. The interior of the apple was as <u>white as snow</u>.

_____

14. The look in her eyes was as <u>cold as ice</u>.

_____

15. The mighty castle was as <u>old as the earth itself</u>.

_____

16. Hurrying here and there, the stonemason was as <u>busy as a beaver</u>.

_____

For additional help, review pages 426–429 in your textbook or visit www.voyagesinenglish.com.

LESSON 5

Limericks

The structure of a **limerick** follows exact rules, but the result is fun and easy to remember.

Circle the letter of the choice that correctly completes each statement.

1. Limericks are best described as
   a. poems that tell sad stories.
   b. poems about nature.
   c. silly rhymes that tell stories.
   d. real-life narratives.

2. Limericks usually feature all the following except
   a. fantastic characters.
   b. real people.
   c. surprising situations.
   d. humorous conclusions.

3. Limericks are probably a commonly used poetic form because they are
   a. easy to write.
   b. short, fun, and easy to remember.
   c. based on true stories.
   d. stories with a moral.

4. To find rhymes for a limerick, a poet might use
   a. an atlas.
   b. an encyclopedia.
   c. a dictionary.
   d. a rhyming dictionary.

Use syllable stress marks to identify the stressed and unstressed syllables in each line. Circle the line if it contains an example of anapestic rhythm.

5. There was an odd, damp odor.

6. She liked to collect ants.

7. "Won't you live in my shoe?"

8. Everyday they bought oranges.

9. Each morning at dawn.

10. He robbed the young man of defeat.

Underline the word that does not rhyme in each set and replace it with a word that does.

11. screwdriver, conniver, survivor, quiver   _____

12. bombastic, postmaster, gymnastic, elastic   _____

13. brother, our, power, shower   _____

14. chore, order, floor, oar   _____

15. quicker, heretic, lunatic, dirty trick   _____

For additional help, review pages 430–433 in your textbook or visit www.voyagesinenglish.com.

Chapter 6 • 159

LESSON

1

What Makes Good Expository Writing?

Expository writing provides factual information. Its purpose is to inform, explain, or define something to its audience. One kind of expository writing is the expository article.

Answer the questions.

1. What should a reader expect to learn from an expository article?

   _____

   _____

2. What should be included in the introduction of an expository article?

   _____

   _____

3. How are the subtopics often organized in the body of an expository article?

   _____

   _____

4. Should the writer include mostly facts or opinions in an expository article? Why?

   _____

   _____

5. What is the purpose of the conclusion of an expository article?

   _____

6. How do the details for an expository article differ from its main idea?

   _____

   _____

7. How might a writer gather details to support the main idea?

   _____

   _____

8. What may cause a writer's main idea to change as he or she gathers details?

   _____

   _____

For additional help, review pages 452–455 in your textbook or visit www.voyagesinenglish.com.

Fact and Opinion

Facts are statements that can be proved true or false. **Opinions** are statements that tell what someone believes. In an expository article, opinions should be avoided unless they are those of experts.

Write *fact* or *opinion* to identify each statement. Circle the opinion signal words.

1. The American tree sparrow is common to Alaska and northern Canada. _____

2. The amazing physicist Gwyn Jones used motorcycle parts in her work. _____

3. In 1794 Eli Whitney patented the cotton gin. _____

4. Women give chocolate to men on Valentine's Day in Japan. _____

5. In a charming return, men give women gifts a month later on White Day. _____

6. A tractor-drawn aerial is a fascinating type of fire truck that has a separate steering mechanism for the rear wheels. _____

7. Concerns over security have triggered proposed legislation requiring online sites with photographic maps to blur out public buildings. _____

8. The Akashi-Kaikyo Bridge is the world's longest suspension bridge. _____

Write one fact and one opinion about each topic.

9. an occupation

   Fact: _____

   Opinion: _____

10. a recent school event

    Fact: _____

    Opinion: _____

11. an animal kept as a pet

    Fact: _____

    Opinion: _____

Cross out the statement that is least relevant to an essay about a mosquito control program.

12. There are approximately 3,500 species of mosquitoes.

13. Mosquitoes are the most deadly disease carriers known, killing millions of people each year.

14. Mosquitoes go through four stages in their life cycle: egg, larva, pupa, and adult.

15. Mosquitoes lay their eggs near open sources of water.

For additional help, review pages 456–459 in your textbook or visit www.voyagesinenglish.com.

Chapter 7 • 161

Noun and Verb Suffixes

A **suffix** is a syllable or syllables added to the end of a word to change its meaning. Suffixes may create nouns or verbs when added to other words.

Complete each sentence by adding a noun suffix to the word in parentheses.

1. The boxes in the _____ need to be labeled and stacked. (base)

2. For your own _____, please be sure your seatbelt is securely fastened. (safe)

3. After living in Iowa for most of her life, Liz is now a _____ of Arizona. (reside)

4. The enthusiastic audience gave a standing ovation to the _____. (piano)

5. Because the hotel had no _____, we had to keep driving. (vacant)

6. Their _____ has endured over the years. (friend)

7. The woman peered through the _____ as she tried to locate the light switch. (dark)

8. Joan valued her job as the _____ to the foundation's president. (assist)

9. By claiming an _____, Randolph received a substantial tax refund. (exempt)

10. Miles suddenly became aware of the _____ of his situation. (real)

Write a new word by adding a verb suffix to each word. Then write a sentence for the new word.

11. soft _____

    _____

12. active _____

    _____

13. computer _____

    _____

14. terror _____

    _____

15. less _____

    _____

16. real _____

    _____

LESSON 4

Quotations

Direct quotations are a person's exact words, either spoken or in print, that are incorporated into your own writing.

Circle the number of each sentence that is correct. Add the correct punctuation and capitalization to the sentences that are incorrect.

1. I regret that I have but one life to give for my country wrote Nathan Hale.

2. Socrates believed that "wisdom begins in wonder."

3. The teacher said explain the proverb the road to a friend's house is never long.

4. "Where there is love there is life," said Mahatma Gandhi.

5. Ralph Waldo Emerson said People only see what they are prepared to see.

6. Quinn asked me what Francis Bacon meant when he said, "Knowledge is power."

7. If you judge people, you have no time to love them Mother Teresa proclaimed.

8. My father likes this quotation by Mark Twain: "You cannot depend on your eyes when your imagination is out of focus."

9. You're happiest while you're making the greatest contribution, said Robert F. Kennedy.

10. The future declared Eleanor Roosevelt belongs to those who believe in the beauty of their dreams.

11. My instructor said, When I start to worry, I remember Nichiren Daishonen's words: No one can avoid problems, not even saints or sages

Write a sentence using each direct quotation.

12. Hope is the dream of a man awake. —French Proverb

_____

13. He who has imagination without learning has wings and no feet. —Joseph Joubert

_____

_____

14. A friend is one who knows you and loves you just the same. —Elbert Hubbard

_____

15. A person who never made a mistake never tried anything new. —Albert Einstein

_____

_____

16. Happiness depends upon ourselves. —Aristotle

_____

© Loyola Press. Voyages in English   Grade 7

For additional help, review pages 464–467 in your textbook or visit www.voyagesinenglish.com.

Chapter 7 • 163

LESSON
5

Library and Internet Sources

When researching information, two of the most efficient ways of finding information are to use references from the **library and Internet sources.**

Write the letter to match each library reference or Internet source to its description.

1. _____ a periodical
2. _____ *Reader's Guide*
3. _____ a .org site
4. _____ an atlas
5. _____ a .com site
6. _____ an encyclopedia
7. _____ a .edu site
8. _____ an almanac or a yearbook
9. _____ a .mil site
10. _____ a .gov site

a. a Web site developed by an organization
b. something published at regular intervals
c. articles on specific topics arranged alphabetically
d. maps and other geographic information
e. listings of magazine articles
f. a military Web site
g. a government Web site
h. a commercial Web site
i. a Web site developed by a school
j. annual facts, statistics, and news items

Circle the letters of the two Web sites that would likely provide the most reliable information for each topic.

11. the number of Congressional state representatives for Massachusetts
    a. a .gov site for the U.S. Congress
    b. a .com site with educational games
    c. a .org site of nonprofit lobbyists
    d. a .org site for Massachusetts history

12. the meaning and etymology of a word
    a. a .edu site from a prominent university
    b. a .com site of a respected print dictionary
    c. a .com dictionary with numerous ads
    d. a .com site to which anyone can contribute articles or information

13. the life of President Lincoln
    a. a .gov site about Illinois history
    b. a .com site selling books about Lincoln
    c. a .gov site about former U.S. presidents
    d. a .org site about American presidents

List three library resources you could use to research the topic. Then list three keywords you might use to find information on the Internet.

Topic: the history of the Alamo

Resources: _____

Keywords: _____

© Loyola Press. Voyages in English   Grade 7

For additional help, review pages 468–471 in your textbook or visit www.voyagesinenglish.com.

What Makes a Good Research Report?

A **research report** explores a specific idea about a topic. Facts are gathered by researching sources such as interviews, books, encyclopedias, almanacs, magazines, newspapers, maps, and documents on the Internet.

Circle the letter of the answer that correctly completes each sentence.

1. The purpose of a research report is to
   a. entertain.
   b. inform.
   c. explain how to do something.

2. The tone of a research report is
   a. formal.
   b. informal.
   c. humorous.

3. A Works Cited page lists
   a. topics.
   b. details.
   c. sources.

4. A thesis statement presents the
   a. main idea.
   b. sources used.
   c. conclusion.

5. Details that support the thesis statement are grouped into
   a. graphics.
   b. subtopics.
   c. topics.

6. Information in a research report should
   a. come from friends.
   b. be in a table of contents.
   c. have several sources.

Read each thesis statement and write two kinds of sources that may provide information for the thesis.

7. Zwickau, Germany, is both an ancient city and a modern one.

   _____

8. Yesterday, the new library in our town was dedicated, making it easier for more people to gain free access to books and research materials.

   _____

9. What could be a more worthwhile way to spend your spring break than by helping build affordable housing?

   _____

10. The development of agriculture led to significant changes in human behavior.

   _____

© Loyola Press. Voyages in English   Grade 7

For additional help, review pages 490–493 in your textbook or visit www.voyagesinenglish.com.

Gathering and Organizing Information

Using note cards is one way to **gather and organize information.** Write on the note cards important details that relate to your topic. At the bottom of the card, write the source and page number.

Complete a note card listing at least three facts for each passage.

The Republic of Indonesia is a country that spans the Asian and Australian continents. It is made up of 17,508 islands, although only 6,000 of those islands are inhabited. 237 million people live in Indonesia. Only three other countries have more people: China, India, and the United States. Indonesia has an elected legislature and a president. Indonesia has a diverse collection of ethnic, linguistic, and religious groups.
—<u>Indonesia</u> by Heather Juno, page 115

The Asian, or Asiatic, elephant is one of the three living elephant species. These are the largest living land animals in Asia and are considered endangered. Asian elephants are often domesticated for use in forestry, tourism, and special occasions and ceremonies. Asian elephants are smaller than African elephants. They can be distinguished by their smaller ears and more slightly rounded back. The tip of their trunk has only one finger-like muscle instead of two.
—<u>Walking Thunder</u> by Steve Smith, page 18

For additional help, review pages 494–497 in your textbook or visit www.voyagesinenglish.com.

LESSON 3

Citing Sources

By **citing your sources** for the reader, you give credit to the source of each fact, idea, or quotation you find. It also tells the reader where to look for more information on the topic.

Write the type of information that is missing from each citation.

1. Book:

   Coville, Jayne. *Cooking with French Chefs*. Baton Rouge, LA: _____, 2001.

2. Encyclopedia:

   _____. *The Encyclopaedia Britannica*. 2010 edition.

3. Web site:

   Sciacca, Mark. "Antique Cars." 2 Dec. 2009 _____.

Write *encyclopedia*, *book*, or *Web site* to identify the source of each citation.

4. "Jane Austin." *World Book*. 2010 ed. _____

5. Macaulay, David. *Castle*. New York, NY: Houghton Mifflin, 1977. _____

6. "Branches of Government." 25 Mar. 2009
   <http://bensguide.gpo.gov/6-8/government/branches.html>. _____

7. "The Great Salt Lake." *New Book of Knowledge*. 2008 edition. _____

8. Symes, Dr. R. F., Dr. R. R. Harding. *Crystal and Gem*.
   New York, NY: DK Publishing, 1991. _____

9. "Why I Am Opposed to the War in Vietnam." 16 Apr. 1967,
   King, Jr., Martin Luther<http://www.hpol.org/record.php?id=150>. _____

10. Porter, Robert. "Ankle Injuries."
    Encyclopedia of Medicine. 2004 ed. _____

Circle the letter of the choice that best completes each statement.

11. Parenthetical notation is
    a. identifying which source a fact comes from.   c. identifying the Web site.
    b. identifying the type of source.   d. identifying the thesis of the report.

12. Plagiarism is
    a. listing the sources in the wrong order.   c. using someone's ideas as your own.
    b. including facts that don't support the topic.   d. using parenthetical notation.

For additional help, review pages 498–501 in your textbook
or visit www.voyagesinenglish.com.

Chapter 8 • 167

LESSON 4

Varied Sentences

Variety is one key to crafting engaging writing with an original voice. Create variety by changing the length, the type, and the structure of your sentences.

Write *natural* or *inverted* to indicate the order of each sentence. Then rewrite the sentence in the opposite order.

1. Above the ocean soared several seagulls. _____

_____

2. The angry bull paced around the circular corral. _____

_____

3. Hovering over her young is the mother deer. _____

_____

4. On the hill overlooking the farm are packs of coyotes. _____

_____

5. Racing through the streets were throngs of runners. _____

_____

Rewrite each sentence as either interrogative or exclamatory. Modify the structure and add or change words if needed.

6. Students will begin the spring-cleanup campaign on Monday.

_____

7. The fireworks finale continued for five minutes uninterrupted.

_____

Rewrite each sentence to begin with a modifier.

8. Jan lifted the boulder with the help of her brother.

_____

9. The city streets look like a spider web on the map.

_____

10. The tiger crouched in its cage waiting for food.

_____

© Loyola Press. Voyages in English Grade 7

For additional help, review pages 502–505 in your textbook or visit www.voyagesinenglish.com.

Denotation and Connotation

A word's **denotation** is its dictionary definition. A word's **connotation** is the implied meaning of the word. Often it suggests a positive or negative value to a word.

Complete the chart by writing an appropriate word. Use a dictionary or thesaurus if you need help.

	POSITIVE CONNOTATION	NEGATIVE CONNOTATION	DENOTATION
1.	anticipation		expectation
2.	lingers	loiters	
3.		nag	horse
4.	moist		damp
5.	scent		smell
6.	converse	chatter	
7.		cowardly	shy
8.		pester	annoy

Rewrite each sentence using neutral words more appropriate for a research report.

9. The Cardinals' efforts fell short of the mark, and the Yankees won 6–3.

_____

10. The new mall will require destroying more than 85 homes in the area.

_____

11. The unproven governor had to make difficult decisions only two weeks into his term.

_____

12. Individuals who gambled in the stock market found themselves suddenly with little to no retirement funds.

_____

_____

13. Gaunt models teetered on spindly shoes as they careened down the walkway.

_____

_____

For additional help, review pages 506–509 in your textbook or visit www.voyagesinenglish.com.